20K A DAY

HOW TO LAUNCH MORE BOOKS AND MAKE MORE MONEY BY WRITING FASTER, BETTER, AND SMARTER

JONATHAN GREEN

Edited by
ALICE FOGLIATA

SERVE NO MASTER: BOOK 3

Paperback Edition ISBN: 978-1539302551

Hardback Edition ISBN: 978-1947667051

To my children Ares and Venus

CONTENTS

FREE GIFT

Thank you so much for buying 20K a Day. As my way of welcoming you to the family, I have a special gift for you. This is a long book and I put together a Top Secret Cheatsheet with all the most valuable information. You can grab it by clicking this link.

ServeNoMaster.com/cheatsheet

WELCOME TO THE 20K REVOLUTION

I think it all comes down to motivation. If you really want to do something, you will work hard for it.
- Sir Edmund Hillary

Lighting Up the Bat Signal

It's four in the morning, and my phone rings.

"Jonathan, it's an emergency. We need your help! Our business partners have invested hundreds of thousands of dollars in our new product launch, and our writer let us down."

All I can say to him is, "Why did you call me at four in the morning about a book? Surely this can wait til the morning?"

"The book goes live in 72 hours. We need something to sell, or we are going to lose all our relationships, and people will lose massive amounts of money. They've invested in advertising for all these campaigns. Everything is already put together. You're the only one who can do it, and we are going to pay you a huge amount of money when you get it done."

Write Fast, Get Paid

Being able to write 35,000 words in less than three days is a unique skill set, and it's one of the things that separates me from most other writers. I get calls from people offering me huge sums of money as a ghostwriter because I can do something no one else can do.

In this book, I'm going to show you exactly how I accomplish that very task. I will take you on a journey that will show you how to become an efficient and highly paid writer in a very short amount of time. On average, I write around 20,000 words a day, without suffering through eight-hour shifts.

My measurement of success is from the beginning to the end of the project, and the average ghostwriting project requires 35,000 words. I like to get those done working two hours a day in a Monday through Friday stretch; in about ten hours of writing, I can crank out those 35,000 words.

Now, with this desperate emergency project, I have to write, edit, finalize everything, and send it to their formatter with enough time for it to be ready for their big launch.

This was not an Amazon book; it was a direct marketing book. In the direct marketing or direct response world, things are formatted a little differently. Books sell for a lot more; instead of $2 or $7, this book was going to sell for $47-$67.

The Busy Writer

I always get offered more jobs than I can handle, and I have a job right now that I'm behind on. I don't have time to do it, but it's in the queue. There is always a list of jobs that I have lined up.

I never have to worry about finding work as a writer. I am very diversified, and while I make a living from selling books on Amazon, I also write books for many direct response companies. I sell some training courses directly through my website, but I also make a great deal of money as a ghostwriter.

Average Joe

Now you probably think that I am the greatest writer in the world and that I have this incredible level of talent. But the truth is, I'm not a very good writer. I consider myself average, at best.

One of my friends is a wonderful writer. He's so talented that it makes me very envious, and very rarely am I a jealous person. When I see someone write at his level, I think, "If I could write like this, more people would connect with my message."

He writes 500 words a week. In the time I've known him, he has finished one book and half of another. In the same time, I have completed over fifty projects.

Quantity is a quality all of its own.

It is important for you to find the balance between speed and quality. If you write fast and the book sucks, it's not going to do you any good.

First Impressions

There are plenty of writers who approach me wanting to work for me or work on a project together, and then I find a grammatical mistake in the first sentence of the sample they send me. They send stuff riddled with errors.

I make a lot of grammatical mistakes in my rough drafts; we all do it. I am not saying I'm perfect, but I would never send out a writing sample without doing the grammar check first.

Three Fears

As a demonstration of what I can do, I am going to take you on a journey. In this book, I'm going to show you how to write even faster than I write. I'm going to share some very amazing and exciting things that can change your destiny.

The three biggest issues writers face are the fear that you're a terrible writer, the fear that you're too slow, and the fear that when you do write something, no one wants to read it. Those are the three limitations that hold everyone back.

We can't cover all three in detail in this book, but I do want to give you a very real experience. I am writing this book in a different way than every book I've written before.

Shattering My Comfort Zone

I've written all my previous books by hand, and when I say I write 35,000 words in a week, that's me sitting in front of my computer typing. But this morning as I was going through the outline for this book and thinking about my strategy, I realized that I need to go outside of my comfort zone.

Every week I generate an enormous amount of audio content. I sit out on the same dock every morning around 5 AM and record podcast episodes. I produce a podcast five days a week.

As I sat out on the dock on the topical island I live on, I thought to myself that I should dictate a book as I've never done that before.

I've dictated on smaller projects and for some of the books I've written in the past, I've dictated a few chapters here and there. I use Dragon Dictate. It's the only real option for dictation software on your computer.

There's a transition period where you have to learn to dictate to your computer. At the end of every sentence, you have to speak the punctuation. The transition and learning period can slow you down. Writing that way breaks my flow because I am constantly correcting mistakes and going back to fix punctuation. That is one part of the dictating process that annoys me.

Pushing Boundaries

The transition period of learning to dictate into my computer slows me down too much. Every word I write generates money and controls my revenue. I make my entire living from what I write and what I say. My whole business and my entire life's work comes from my ability to write books, so slowing down for a month or six weeks to learn this software is going to cost me loads of money in lost time and lost opportunity.

Sitting on the Dock of the Bay

I live on this tropical island, and I want to be outside all the time. Sitting inside writing on my computer is a little bit depressing, so why not write outside instead?

While sitting here watching these incredible waves and enjoying the blazing sun on my back, I am recording this book outside right now. Usually, I don't record audio during the day because I'm worried about background noise, but I'm not recording an audiobook. I can edit this later myself.

I don't know how the final process of creating this book will go. There are two possibilities for how I will convert this audio into text. I will either use Dragon Dictate to transcribe, and then I'll have to go through and edit all the punctuation myself, or I'll use a professional transcriptionist, and they will transcribe everything and add in all the punctuation.

Those are the two choices now.

Transcription Secret

One little piece of advice when using a transcriptionist: they charge per minute. When I'm recording this, I have these long pauses where I am thinking for a few seconds. Those spaces are wasted time because I'm paying for the transcriptionist by the minute. They charge me whether I'm saying anything or not.

You can use a tool like Audacity to remove those silences. It's called "truncating the silence." I have some screenshots on the 20K page showing exactly how I do it. You don't want to go overboard if people are going to listen to your recording. This effect can make the audio sound very choppy and will annoy anyone listening, but you can save yourself 20 to 30 percent of the cost of having someone transcribe your book.

Now I don't want to share that secret with my transcriber because they will be annoyed. So there's an excellent chance that I'll transcribe this part using Dragon so that she never finds out about my little secret.

What You Will Learn

I'm excited to have you with me on this journey. Anytime someone buys a book from me or grabs it via Kindle Unlimited (or maybe you even stole it) it means a lot to me; it means a lot that you're trusting me to help you develop a critical skill. We are walking down this path together.

You're going to learn how to accomplish some amazing things. The faster you can write, the more money you make. It's the simplest formula in the world. As you progress as a writer from getting paid per word to getting paid percentages of your projects, your growth transforms from arithmetic to geometric. Instead of going in a straight line, your income looks like a rocket ship flying up a parabola.

When you are faster, the benefit is greater when you're a percentage writer. One of the books I wrote and edited over the course of thirty-five hours generated over $70,000 in commissions for me.

That was the first book I ever wrote for someone else, and that's when I realized that writing is fantastic and writing fast is even better. That project paid so much money for so little work. That's when I fell in love with writing.

I'm going to show you everything that I do: the exact process that I use to write amazing and brilliant books. Thank you so much for joining me on this journey, and I can't wait to meet you at the finish line.

Additional Content

As you've already noticed, I just can't fit everything I want to share with you in this book. For that reason, I've created a page on my website loaded to the gills with free additional information.

ServeNoMaster.com/20K

Any time I talk about pictures I've taken from my dock, blogging about my book creation process, or links to software that I use, you can find it on this page. This is the central hub for all the additional material for breaking the 20K a Day barrier.

Who Am I?

Before we go any further, I'd like to give you a chance to get to know me, an opportunity to understand who I am and where I come from.

Why should you listen to me? Why should you trust me when it comes to writing?

You deserve to have those questions answered. Anytime you go to someone for advice or wisdom, it's important to know that the person is an expert at what they do. In reality, I'm not much of a writing teacher, and I'm not much of a writing coach.

That's not really how I make my living. I make my living as a writer, and I decided to launch this project on the side just six months ago. I built a website called Serve No Master and began creating products and writing blog posts and starting a podcast.

I started this side project as a hobby because I want to teach more people how to have the same life that I have.

I live on a tiny tropical island. Right now, I'm looking at crystal blue water and incredible waves. I can't see a single human in front of me. If I turn all the way to the right, there's one person on the beach about 250 meters away. If I look to my left, I don't see anybody. There might be people directly behind me, but I can't see them when I turn my head.

All I can see are beautiful waves and amazing clouds.

(I have placed photos from each of my writing sessions at ServeN-oMaster.com/20k – including the magical day of the triple rainbow. I will be posting all links and extended content on this page.)

I live in the tropics in the South Pacific on this amazing island. All my dreams have come true because of my ability to write fast, and I want to pass that ability on to you. Now that I've achieved all my goals, it's time for me to pay it forward and help other people reach their dreams because that makes me feel magnificent.

I've always struggled with different types of adversity in my life. People often tell me that I can't do the things I want to do. When I graduated from my master's program in London, there were thirty other teachers in the program. Twenty-nine other high school teachers surrounded me, and they all said they wanted to complete this degree so that they could get a 5 percent raise back at their old jobs.

When I said, "That doesn't interest me. I'm here because I want to start teaching at university level," every one of them said that was impossible. That no one would hire me because I was just twenty-nine years old. That you can't teach at a university with just a master's degree; you need a doctorate degree. They said all these things, and four months later every single one of them was teaching at their old positions at small high schools around the world. I was teaching and running a department at the seventeenth best university in the United States at the time.

Eventually, that job fell apart. It turned out it was the wrong move for me, and my boss fired me after just thirteen magical days. When they fired me, they spoke words of death over my career and said that I would never be successful again, that my life was over.

They didn't just want to fire me; they wanted to sentence me to a life of poverty. And this is how some people get fired; sometimes your bosses are sad to let you go, and they are very nice as they show you the door, but sometimes bosses hate you and want to destroy your life for the rest of eternity.

I got one of those enjoyable firings.

When people tell me that I can't achieve something, it becomes my obsession. That was my motivation as I built my online business, and over the past seven years, I've made far more money than the boss who fired me will make in her entire lifetime.

I've shattered some incredible goals. People also told me that I could never write a best-selling novel. Having written more than fifty, I've reached that goal so many times that it no longer interests me. I often don't even tell people that I'm a bestselling author because it's not exciting to me anymore. I've hit that goal, and when you hit a target a certain number of times, it's not very exciting to you anymore.

Now I have a new goal. My new mission is about the Serve No Master brand, these books, and everything, including all the free training on my website. All this content, it's all about one single goal, and that is to prove that I can replicate what I do in you.

People told me that I couldn't be a bestseller, then they said I couldn't teach other people to do it.

Challenge accepted.

My goal is to teach you to become a fast and successful writer. Having worked in multiple markets and written books in so many different spaces with bestsellers across the spectrum, I have no doubt that if you follow my system and if you finish this book, you will achieve greatness.

I've made well into seven figures from my book writing. Books that I've written have grossed over $10 million. That includes direct response and books that have sold on Amazon. I think that's a whole lot of money.

I'm not the best writer in the world, and there are plenty of writers who have sold more books and made more money than me. What matters to me and what I'm excited about, is the ratio of time worked to money earned.

Right now, I'm sitting on my little dock watching crabs play on the rocks and enjoying the sunshine and being in paradise. It's not just about what you do; it's how you do it.

I know plenty of writers who grind in a basement in a nightmare situation, writing and writing and writing. Is it worth it to make more money if you have to work that many hours? It doesn't sound very exciting to me.

When I think about your future, I want you to be someone who writes just two to four hours a day and spends the rest of your day with your children, your family, and the ones you love.

At whatever phase you are in life, I want you to accomplish amazing things, and I want to hear about it. I love all the emails I get from people who read my books, visit my website, and listen to my podcast. That's very exciting for me, and it means a lot to me that people reach out. I respond to every single email I get personally.

Every email starts with the writer wanting to see if I reply. I always get that same message, and I always reply myself. When we start having these amazing conversations, it's precious to me. I love connecting with people who have gained from what I share.

Together we're taking this incredible journey. I will not only help you to replicate some of my skills but also to develop the life you want. Not everybody wants to live on a tropical island like I do.

All you need to build a writing career now is a smartphone and a microphone. You don't even need a laptop anymore, just get other people to edit your book.

I am going to show you some cool secrets. As you get a little farther into this book, I have some exciting things that I can't wait to share with you.

WHAT'S THIS BOOK ABOUT?

My parents always taught me that my day job would never make me rich; it'd be my homework.
    - Daymond John

Hitting Big Numbers

People frequently message me to ask questions about writing fast, keeping the story going, and deciding what to write about.

When people reach out to me about the same thing multiple times, that's a sign that it's an important topic to cover.

Rather than placing the same information in email after email, I decided to create this book to provide a single resource that I could point people to.

This book is designed to meet you exactly where you need help. It can help you to accomplish several important things. I want to help you increase your writing speed, and I want to help you increase your endurance. I'm going to help improve your book production process.

Throughout this book, we will focus on one core principle: speed. Being able to write fast is a wonderful skill. As you learn to write more words per minute, you will create a greater endurance for writing.

What good is writing 5,000 words an hour if you get burned out after thirty minutes?

Words per hour becomes an artificial number if you aren't writing for multiple hours every single day. We are going to work together to create something that is sustainable. New writers often make the mistake of pushing themselves too hard and burning themselves out.

There's a moment when you're writing and when you just feel a sense of exhaustion. For me, when I'm working on a massive project of 10 or 20,000 words, I suddenly notice the quality of what I'm writing is beginning to diminish. I can feel the quality going down and the mistakes going up. I'm very tempted to push through, especially if I'm at 17,000 words.

I always want to have a 20,000-word day, but when you push too hard, you hurt yourself the next day. The next day you can't recover as quickly because you are tired and worn out. If you push yourself too far and burn out, then your quality of work the next day goes down.

Suddenly you can only write half as long the next day.

You must develop a pace that is maintainable. As much as writing is about small sprints, it's also about marathons of writing large blocks of words every day. When you have these structures in place and can write a large number of words per hour, you know what you're capable of. That helps you plan out your projects much more efficiently.

Very rarely do I spend entire days writing. I like to spend part of the day writing and part of the day working on other projects. While dictating this book, I'm also working on several other projects at the same time. I don't want to spend eight hours a day writing.

I don't know if it will take me even eight hours to dictate this entire book (It didn't. It only took seven hours and thirty-six minutes.), but I'm going to dictate this book in one-hour blocks. Each section I record is a different audio file. And each dictation session is roughly forty to sixty minutes.

Dictating a book is an entirely new system for me; therefore, I don't know how long this entire process will take. I'm learning how much I can handle. I do know that if I dictate for too long, I will damage my voice and hurt my throat. And if that happens, I won't be able to perform for several days.

Many of the stories and the lessons in this guide come from my personal experiences and not just opinion and speculation.

The ability to write fast, capacity to write for longer spaces of time, and knowing your endurance limits, puts you in control of your destiny and can unlock the ability to make a living from your writing.

This Book Has Homework?

You'll notice that this book is loaded with little sections called "Action Steps." These steps weren't actually my idea. One of my wonderful Tribe members came up with the idea when he read an early draft of the book. They are exercises that he devised for himself after reading each section.

Less than a week after reading the rough draft of this book, he had nearly written 20,000 words and finished his first book. The exercises are really working for him and I'm excited to share them with you.

One of the best things you can do is take some notes in a special notebook while you go through this book. There will be loads of information that you simply absorb, but there will also be a few gems that you really want to latch on to. I keep two notebooks with me at all times to store ideas and plan out all my projects. Feel free save the action steps in your notebook. And yes, I know that some of the action steps are just really good notes. They are still worth saving!

There are often questions in the action steps as well. Don't just copy them into your notebook; write down your answers.

Action Steps

1 Remember: our goal is to write books fast that sell.

2. Write daily. Even if you only write five minutes a day, you are establishing a powerful habit.

THE FIRST DICTATION

Do not be embarrassed by your failures, learn from them and start again.
- Richard Branson

The Sport of Writing

The real key to success with any project, but especially with writing, is your foundation.

There is a dreaded moment every author faces when they are sitting in front of a blank page and can't figure out what to write. As an author, you get hit with this massive hammer of writer's block, and it's the worst feeling in the world.

Writer's block becomes stronger the more you think about it. The condition continues to get worse and worse because an aberration became something we thought was real and we started getting more and more worried about it.

This is what happens when you mix up random error with systemic error.

A CRITICAL LESSON - The Two Types of Errors

Random error is when you run into a series of different problems. A systemic error is when you run into the exact same problem over and over again.

Random Errors

We often blame random errors on an act of God or the universe. If you write several books and the first book has a ton of spelling problems, the second book has something wrong with the cover, and the third book no one wants to give a positive review, you start to think the universe is against you. You say that you're cursed, but in reality, you are showing signs of improvement as a writer because each time you have a different problem.

When you make a mistake, you learn from it so you don't repeat it. You move up the mountain from good to great.

The ability to understand that some problems are random and to learn from them guarantees you will become successful.

When we turn that random error of "I can't think of anything to write about today" into a big problem called writer's block, we treat it like a systemic problem.

The way to conquer systemic problems is to isolate the cause and eradicate them at the root.

Research Kills Writer's Block

The best way to avoid writer's block is never to let it happen in the first place. I've never sat in front my computer and stared at a blank page for hours. It's not that I'm a great writer, but I am an excellent researcher.

The foundation of a successful book, whether it's fiction, nonfiction, or a cookbook, is preparation. For every hour you spend researching, you can shave as many as ten hours from your writing process. This entire book was extensively outlined long before I started recording the first word.

A phenomenal amount of research went into this book. I went and looked at how other people write fast and how they talk about writing so that I could see their approaches. To look for other ideas that are different from my method because there are many different ways to learn to do everything. There are loads of martial arts you can learn, but in the end, they all teach you the same thing: how to fight.

There are a lot of different ways to write fast, but I'm sharing with you the technique that works for me and the method that will work for you. It all starts with a sturdy foundation.

Some people approach writing fiction with no plan and no outline. Some people are very successful using this method. They are the minority, but they exist. As with anything, there's always someone who can do something different.

Some people are double-jointed, and some people can speak twenty languages, but it doesn't mean that anyone can learn to do it. I would never write a book without an outline.

It's impossible for me to do and it's certainly impossible to do it fast. Your brain has two modes: there is the mode where you are absorbing information and the mode where you are pushing information out. Research is an absorbing phase and writing is a pushing-out phase; you're taking the content and the ideas from within your mind and putting them out on paper.

When you research and try to think of ideas on the fly, you keep switching back and forth between these modes, and it's not a quick transition. You lose massive amounts of time to this inefficiency.

I can write 1,000 words in two hours if I'm researching at the same time. Doing both at the same time slows down my research and how fast I write. It ruins both sides of the equation. Before we continue, if there's one thing I want you take away from this book, it's for you to understand the importance of outlining and deep research before you start writing.

Scaffolding

Proper research and outlining will change everything for you. Even if you're already doing well as a writer, you will become significantly faster.

I enjoy adult coloring books because they make art simple.

With a coloring book, you have all the lines, and you know to fill in these clearly defined spaces with different colors. The book gives you structure. Coloring books are art with training wheels or scaffolding. Like bowling with the bumpers.

If I give you a very intricate design of shapes on a piece of paper, you can color it and make it look beautiful. However, if I give you a blank piece of paper and ask you to accomplish the same thing, you will fail unless you are an amazing artist.

Using scaffolding in many areas of life is acceptable, but for some reason, we think that in artistic areas it's a sign of weakness or laziness. It's silly to think that way.

The first phase of writing a book is to create the deepest outline you can accomplish. I go extensively into how to research in my book *Breaking Orbit*. That book is a lot about my research methodology.

This book isn't about research; it is about writing fast. But good research is the foundation for writing fast.

In just a moment, I will share with you a couple of secrets and techniques, but if you need me to go even deeper into outlining and research, head over to my blog. I cover this extensively in several blog posts and podcast episodes, as well as in *Breaking Orbit*.

I don't want to force you to read the same material over and over again about my researching process, but I want to give you an overview so you can replicate on a basic level my structure for preparing to write fast.

Action Steps

1 Remember that it's ok to use scaffolding as an artist

2. What is the difference between random and systemic error?

3. Should you blame your success or lack of success on luck?

MY WRITING HISTORY

Time is my greatest enemy.
  - Evita Peron

How I Sprint

We are going to talk a great deal about writing sprints in this book. When you first start sprinting, you will write for five-minute blocks. In these sessions, you write as much as you can without worrying about mistakes.

Many writers find that small sprints interspersed with small breaks are their ideal writing rhythm. Small sprints are a great way to start and build up your writing stamina, but they are not how I write. Five minutes is not nearly enough time for me to get into the zone.

When I hit my stride, I can crank out words for hours at a time without needing a break. I prefer to write until I get tired and then take a longer break. This is true marathon writing, and it's not for the faint of heart. My body determines my finish line, not a stopwatch.

My normal writing rhythm is to take longer breaks when I need them. I don't like to work eight hours straight; that's too much even for me.

I will write between two and four hours in the morning. Then I will spend two to three hours relaxing in the middle of the day. I spend this time working on other projects or enjoying a leisurely lunch. I also have plenty of time to spend with my family.

Later in the afternoon, I'll write for another three to four hours. This allows me to easily hit 20,000 words a day and still enjoy my life. That's the rhythm that currently works well for me.

Starting this Book

We are going to find the rhythm that works perfectly for you. There is no reason to expect our styles to be identical. I'm a raw marathon writer because that is what gets me the best results. We are going to break down some key strategies for maximizing your daily word counts with smaller sprints later in the book.

If you decide to use the sprint method, we can either lengthen sessions or increase the number of sessions to pump up your words per day.

FIRST STEP TO WRITING FASTER

You must take the first step. The first steps will take some effort, maybe pain. But after that, everything that has to be done is real-life movement.
- Ben Stein

Why should I learn to write faster?

When starting a new venture or going through any training course where you are trying to learn a skill, you always want to think about the end result. What's the final benefit for me? Why do I want to go down this path? What is it going to do to help me?

It's very important to go through this step because many of us get shiny object syndrome. We get excited about projects, and we follow a project here and a project there, and then we forget the end goal of that first project.

The Real Goal

You should not be reading this book simply to write fast; that's not why you're reading it. You have a goal that you want to write faster. Writing faster is a means to an end.

We want to think about that secondary goal because that will keep you motivated and ensure that you're one of the people who finishes this book. You will directly apply these principles and becomes a successful writer if we focus correctly.

The first benefit of this book is that you will be able to write faster, and you will be able to accomplish more in less time. That means you can get more done every day. It also means you have more time to spend on other things, whether that is working on other projects or simply spending more time doing the things you love.

The Gift of Life

The more efficient you become with writing, the more of your time you earn back. Time is more valuable than money. When you're 100 years old and you're on your deathbed, you aren't going to ask for more money. You will ask for more time, just like everybody else.

I would rather give you more time right now. If you get just as much writing done in two hours as you are doing in four hours right now, I'm giving you back two hours a day. That's ten hours a week; 520 hours a year is an enormous amount of time to get back! (And that's assuming you only write for four hours a day and take weekends off.)

Giving you back your life is the ultimate gift.

You can spend that time however you like, including growing and expanding your marketing efforts. So much of marketing these days is content marketing, which means creating information. I create blog posts, books, courses, and podcast episodes all to get my message out in the world. That's how I find my audience; having a lot of content for them to consume.

Quantity is a Quality of its Own

This is the third book in the *Serve No Master* series. I have added a second series called the *Habit of Discipline* simply because I write so much that I'm always a step ahead. In this one Amazon channel, I will put out more than twenty books this year.

That is in addition to the books I write for my three other pen names. That is also in addition to the seven other projects I have going on with different partners in the direct response world as well as my podcast and the copywriting work I'm doing now.

Being able to generate a lot of content is very valuable. It allows you to expand quickly. Doubling your writing speed and improving your efficiency also improves your economic situation. Turning that four-hour project into a two-hour project will open up new opportunities.

Fast and Slow Income Streams

When you double your writing speed, you can spend two hours a day writing for your passion project and two hours a day on ghostwriting projects. You can make more money and pursue your dreams at the same time. Having revenue coming in each day will take the stress off you while writing your novel.

That short-term revenue will pay the bills while you build to that first royalty paycheck. You will get more practice writing. The more words you write, the better you get. Having written, published, and sold well over 100 million words, I can look back at my previous books and see how much better I've gotten with every book that I've written.

Keep Getting Better

Books that I wrote two years ago are not nearly as good as books that I write now. They are beautiful, and I'm proud of the work I've accomplished, but my strong marketing made up for my lack of ability while I developed and honed my writing skills.

Most first novels aren't very good, and that's ok. Were you able to tie your shoes the first time you tried? Were you amazing at sports the first time you tried? Of course not.

We develop skills through practice, repetition, and experience. Expecting to hit it out of the park and be perfect the first time you do something is very irrational. We should apply the same rationality to each of our new endeavors, but we don't.

We always assume that the first book we write will be a massive success. We expect that we will write easily, write fast, and find the perfect market without effort. But that's not reality. Nobody starts out perfect.

I'm glad that I can look back and see that my previous works were not as good as what I'm doing now. That means that I'm improving. Better books are not a sign of failure but proof that you are a real writer. Your books will continue to get better.

There is no feeling worse than that of being a fading star.

If this is your first book...you have to write

My improvement is the result of continued writing, even after my first books. The benefit of experience is improvement. The time you spend writing has real value. The faster you write, the sooner you will achieve excellence.

You may have noticed that I'm not the greatest writer in the world. That should inspire you. If someone who writes as poorly as I do can make a living, how much better can someone with your great skill do?

The more you write and the more hours you put in, the more success you can find. There is no other way to learn writing than actually to do it. You can read five books about swimming, but unless you get in the water, you are not going to know what to do.

My daughter is four years old, and she has been swimming for more than half her life. She is trained to always wear a life jacket on the open ocean. We are very serious about water safety, but what good is a life jacket if she doesn't trust and understand it?

To see if she can handle a real emergency, we sometimes throw her into the middle of the pool. It's a controlled situation, but she is still surprised.

Do you want the first time your child tries to swim to be in a real emergency?

Writing is the same. You can read, study, and write stories just for yourself, but until you start writing something that you want to release into the world, that fear isn't there. That real experience is where your iron will get forged.

Zoning Out Distractions

There are other things you can do to improve the quality and speed of your writing. I read a book every single day, and this helps me to think in words instead of just sounds. Reading is just one tool on the path to becoming a great writer, but alone it is not enough. Being able to read does not make me able to write well.

Another big part of writing is getting into the zone, and people give different names to this feeling. Sometimes people will talk about the runner's high; however, I've never run far enough to experience it for myself. The zone for me is where you're writing, and you lose track of time, and you look back and realize that you just wrote 5,000 words in the last thirty or sixty minutes.

It is this incredible state of being where you're writing fast, and you're totally in the zone with your book, and you're not thinking about other things. We constantly face distraction, and it's especially easy to get distracted as a writer. You are working for yourself, and there isn't anybody to check on your work or scold you for slacking off.

You can fire up the television, or you can watch a movie. You can play with your kids or just play video games. You can jump over to any website you want. One click of the mouse and you're watching videos online.

There are so many distractions, but when you get into the zone you lose the desire to interact with them, and you forget that they're there.

Writing in the zone is precious because it's an amazing feeling when you accomplish so much. It's amazing what you can accomplish without it being difficult. The beginning of any new project is the most difficult part for me. The first few pages of a new book are where I always struggle and face the biggest desire to procrastinate.

Writing the first one or 2,000 words, I feel like I'm fighting against myself. But then I hit that spot and I am in the zone. Then it becomes easy.

You're going to learn by the end of this book how to get into the zone every time you have a writing session.

(Editing note: Yesterday, I was editing the first session of this book, and I just couldn't get into the zone. But in three hours I still edited and rewrote over 7,000 words. That was *out* of the zone. This is the kind of speed you can look forward to when you complete the 20K system.)

Writing doesn't need to be hard, and great writing doesn't need to be challenging. With the zone, you can do it in a way that's enjoyable.

Short Goals

The final reason to speed up your writing is to bring the goal or destination closer to you. Many people set a huge goal for their first book of 90 or 200,000 words. They have these massive goals because they want to write books in categories that demand great length.

When your goal is to write a 100,000-word book, and you are only writing 100 words a day, you are nearly three years away from hitting that goal.

It's very hard for us as humans to take the long view. We're very much a short-sighted people. Short-sightedness is why we make so many poor short-term decisions.

This short-sightedness applies to writing just as much as anything else. When the finish line for your book is months away, it's hard to stay the course because it's simply too far away.

I love writing, but I hate running. The thought of running a marathon is a nightmare to me because it takes so long. I don't have the patience for that.

The thought of running for four hours straight (and let's be honest, if I ran a marathon it would be closer to eight hours) is a nightmare to me because it's so far away. However, I can run for twenty minutes without any issues because that's an achievable goal. I could do a 5K in a pinch. I wouldn't be very fast, and I would certainly struggle because running is not one of the sports I do very often.

A closer goal is achievable, but when you have a goal that is two years away, the odds of hitting it trend toward zero. We struggle with goals that are far away in every area of life. I don't like far-away goals. I prefer my goals to be right in front of my face.

I wrote 93,000 words for *Serve No Master* in four days. *Breaking Orbit* is just over 41,000 words, and I wrote that casually over the course of three days and a quick little morning session.

I spent most of those days working on other projects just like I am while writing this book. I'm only spending one to two hours a day recording, and this book will be written in less than a week.

When the finish line is close, achieving total focus is obtainable. How many times have people told you that they operate well under pressure? That they do better with deadlines?

They are expressing this critical core concept. Humans respond to clear and visible goals. If you want to finish your book, then you need to be able to feel the finish line in your bones.

If you can start a book on Monday and finish by Friday, that's a very achievable and manageable task. Suddenly your work output becomes predictable. You can plan for the future and organize your writing schedule. Anyone can handle five days of writing. That's a goal that doesn't feel overwhelming. Instead, it feels accomplishable, and that's what we want.

We want a goal that you feel like you can reach because then you'll reach it. When a goal seems very far away, like it's going to take weeks or months or even years to reach, we lose the course.

It's challenging for us to maintain focus for that long. We start to feel overwhelmed; that far-away goal is too daunting. For some of my coaching clients, their biggest struggle is that they feel like they're never going to hit the finish line. They have been struggling for so long that the goal doesn't feel real.

Man on the Moon

There is only one reason that America put a man on the moon in the 1960s. President Kennedy stood in Rice Stadium in 1962 and said, "We choose to go to the moon in this decade."

This one line from a phenomenal speech changed everything. He set a goal in a workable timeframe.

The Doldrums

With goals, time frame is everything.

When one of my coaching clients has been working on a book for six, twelve or even eighteen months, they reach this moment where they suddenly feel this sense of terror. This sense of impending doom becomes overwhelming.

When we are close to the finish line on a project that took too long, we start to think that it's never going to happen and just decide to quit when we are so close to hitting that goal.

This destroys so many writers. It destroys many entrepreneurs as well. We get to that point, and we are so close to crossing the finish line, but we lose heart, and we give up.

We decide that this is never going to work anyways and we procrastinate more and more. We fail to release the book, or we fail to finish the book. Or we fail to write the final chapter. For everyone, it's a different moment in the process.

For some people, the investment becomes emotional. When you spend three years writing a book, you are so emotionally connected to it that the thought of rejection becomes overwhelming. There is nothing worse than finding out you wasted three years of your life. Better to never release the book and never risk that rejection.

We get stuck in a moment that we hate. Everyone has a part of the writing process that they hate the most. I love researching and writing, but I dread editing. The editing process is where I get bogged down. I will write a book in just a few days, but editing takes me two to four times longer depending on the project.

The Editor's Curse

Getting in the zone for editing is a nightmare for me. It's where the temptation to procrastinate or work on another project rears its ugly little head. Fortunately, I have been massively improving my editing process, and I am going to show you some great stuff later in the book to speed that part up.

Because I hate editing so much, I've gotten very good at it. It doesn't take nearly as long as it did six months ago. Although I'm able to edit much faster, I still don't love it.

Writing is a creative process, and I love creating content. My passion has become my career. But editing uses the logical and analytical part of your brain. It feels like I'm stuck back in school.

With this book, my decision to dictate rather than write by hand means that my editing process will be more extensive. There are a lot more challenges when turning spoken words into written words. I know that editing a dictation is harder.

Right now, I'm sitting on my little dock enjoying life and dictating this book. However, when the time comes to edit the transcriptions, I will pay for all this freedom with longer and tougher editing sessions.

(I was right. Editing a dictation is much harder than any of my previous books.)

With dictation, there are many unique problems. Sometimes I say the wrongs words or the dictation software makes a mistake. I use overly familiar language or spew run-on sentences.

There is a trade-off between dictating and editing, and I'm very interested to see what that experience is like.

Now you know upfront that I don't like editing. That's why I worked to speed up my editing process just as I worked to speed up my writing process. By the end of this book, you will know how to do both, so you can feel closer to your goal.

You can accomplish more and have a better sense of what you can do as a writer. This will give you more confidence and allow you to make more money and build a real business around your writing.

Action Steps

1. Know your end goal.

2. Why do you want to write faster?

3. What are the biggest distractions when you want to write?

4. Establish a strategy to master your distractions one by one.

5. Sit down for a session and write for as long as it takes to get into the writing "zone."

6. Break your big goals down into smaller goals.

THE 20K A DAY TRACKING SYSTEM

This search for what you want is like tracking something that doesn't want to be tracked. It takes time to get a dance right, to create something memorable.

- Fred Astaire

You Must Track Your Progress

Tracking your progress is absolutely, unequivocally the most important step in the 20K Writing System.

You must track your progress with any venture or project. If you don't track your progress, you won't know how well you're doing.

We need a tracking system that allows us to measure our goals. If you don't track how many words you write and just go by feeling, you will fail this process. Because, for instance, you will not know if you go from 2000 words to 2500 words a day. You won't recognize your significant improvement. If you're not tracking your progress, you won't realize you are 25 percent faster. You will feel like this process has failed and you haven't accomplished anything.

Studies show that without tracking, our minds forget where we started. We'll feel a sense of accomplishment, but then we'll forget our progress. We are very at bad remembering what we've done.

In looking back at the past, you don't remember how well you did a week ago.

How do you know if you're doing better today without a written record? You can see this principle in action every day in every gym in the world.

When you go to the gym and lift weights, if you don't write down how much weight you lifted last week, you won't remember just a few days later. The problem is that the action is so repetitive. Your brain isn't going to store a memory that looks just like every other memory you have of the gym.

You are repeating the same memory over and over again; you're pushing that bar above the bench press over and over and over again. You're working so hard and pushing that bar with all that weight, but if you do it three times a week how can you remember what you did seventeen sessions ago?

We don't have a perfect memory. This process of writing fast is objective. It's all about the numbers. Feeling just doesn't matter. Without deep statistics and consistent tracking, you won't notice when you are having problems.

Everyone writes in a different way; some of us are good at writing in the morning, and some are good at writing in the evening. Some people can write for an hour straight, but then they need a break for thirty minutes.

Some people can write for five hours straight without needing a break. Some of us can easily write five days a week but falter when we try to do seven.

We need to find your writing sweet spot, and only with hard data can we find it. You may discover that you like writing in the morning, but you write 10 percent faster in the evening. This information is crucial to planning your writing strategy.

I do a lot of tracking with writing locations, and I regularly experiment on myself. Last year, I had a little office about 200 meters from my house. It was this little concrete box with soundproof walls that I could use to record lots of videos and my other audio work with ease. I was cranking out these massive work sessions and getting into the zone was a breeze.

But then I noticed that I was spending twelve-hour days in my little bunker. We are living in paradise, and I was spending my days in an office without a window.

Now I work out of my bedroom. Although I was able to work efficiently in my little bunker, I would rather give up 10 to 15 percent of my efficiency to be near my children all day. Most of the time when I'm writing, at least one of my kids is in the room with me, and I love that.

Working from home does mean more interruptions and more background noise, but I am willing to overcome these challenges to be able to spend more time with my family.

If working from home decreased my efficiency by 60 or 70 percent, then I wouldn't do it because it would affect my income too much.

Learning to write faster is not artistic. The 20K System is not about your creativity or eloquent writing; this system focuses on the scientific part of writing.

I'm not a very eloquent writer. I am, however, a fast writer, and that's the goal we're focused on. We want to see how many words you can accomplish in our critical timeframes. We want to discover the pattern that works best for you and help you find the best writing strategy for you as an individual and unique writer.

For me, dictating is so much faster than typing, but the editing process is crucial in determining if this is the best strategy for me going forward. I need to measure my writing speed and combine both the writing and entire editing process to see if dictation is faster than writing the whole book by hand.

The Harsh Truths of Tracking Your Progress

Throughout this journey, you need to track your progress. At first, it's easy to be excited about the process, but you will eventually reach a point where you are no longer excited about tracking your work. It can seem repetitive to write down numbers every day.

When you are tempted to skip this step, realize that this will hurt you for the rest of your writing career. If you start fudging numbers, it will slow you down and decrease your effectiveness.

This data is not about impressing anyone; it's about achieving your goals as quickly as possible.

We need to track consistently and efficiently. When you stop tracking, you lose your effectiveness. Every time I stop tracking my numbers, the quality of my workouts diminishes. It's easy to imagine we've done more than we have when we stop tracking our work.

You're going to have good and bad days. When you have a bad day, you may be tempted to not write it down, but don't do that. Having data about your bad writing sessions will help you to diagnose and then fix the cause.

No one's ever going to see your numbers unless you decide to share them. I'm not going to make you email me your numbers, and I'm not going to make you put them somewhere public where people can judge you and see if you had a good or bad day.

Whether my writing is good or bad, I track how many words I write every day. That is the statistic I look at the most.

I don't track my progress through words per hour. Words per hour isn't enough to get you to the finish line.

Sprinting fast is awesome, and if you can write 5,000 words per hour, that's great. But if you're only writing forty minutes a day, that number is meaningless.

Words per hour is sprinting, and words per day is running a marathon. Writing a book is not a sprint, so training as a sprinter will not help you. Knowing your numbers will allow you to estimate when you will finish each project.

Sprinting may be relevant for you if you are writing articles or blog posts. In that case, your measurement is more about how many articles can you write per day.

Knowing how many days it will take me to finish each book allows me to give accurate numbers to publishers and clients. I can estimate when a book will be done and take on the right number of projects so that I have steady work, without feeling overwhelmed.

If you're an article or blog post writer, sprinting will be crucial. You need to know how long it takes you to crank out an article to determine how many assignments you can accept. By knowing this information, you can provide better time estimates and make more accurate job bids.

The more you know your numbers, the easier it will be for you to achieve success as a writer.

Explore with an Open Mind

Not everything is going to work for you. Some of the techniques I'm going to share with you in this book will crash and burn. They will be complete and total failures.

Some of them will improve your writing speed, and some will slow you down. Remember, we're trying to learn a new skill together. There are going to be ups and downs. We might have three or four bad days, but then on day five, you double your writing speed.

Together we are going to find the right workflow for you.

If you incorporate my techniques into your writing, then you have the opportunity to become a faster and more efficient writer. My techniques and writing processes are the result of millions of published words and hours of trial and error.

You can achieve excellence; we just have to work together.

How To Track Your Progress

There are several different ways to track your progress. Each of these different methodologies will work for different people. You may need to try several different techniques to find what works best for you.

There are certain things that I always write by hand. When I create my notes for my podcast episodes, I always write them in a notebook. Then I take my notebook out to the dock where I record.

I don't like the idea of typing up my notes and printing them out or sending them to my iPad, even though that might increase my efficiency. I am a person who sticks with techniques that work for me.

If you are a tactile person, you might enjoy keeping a physical notebook. Buy a special notebook and keep it next to your computer. At the end of every hour, write down how many words you have written and the time.

Notebooks don't work for everyone. You may be a spreadsheets kind of person. I don't use spreadsheets very often, therefore that's not how I track my word counts.

But perhaps you are a statistics person and you enjoy the sight of numbers in rows. Perhaps you're good at Excel. If you were good at math or science in school, then Excel may be the perfect way for you to track your word count.

The key is to find the method that you will stick with.

Word Count Math

You might struggle with knowing how many words you've written in the past hour. Perhaps you can only see the total word count in your document.

All you have to do is write the total word count for your document every hour and then later on you will have to do a little math. Take your word count and subtract the word count from an hour earlier. Your 11 AM total minus your 10 AM total is how many words you wrote during that hour.

If you are great at Excel, you can set up some formulas that do this automatically.

Best Time of the Day to Write

Keep track of each hour you write during the day to monitor your overall efficiency. You might notice that for the first hour you write, you're okay. Then in hours two and three you start to speed up, but at hour four, your work starts slipping. This is really valuable data!

We are learning how long it takes you to warm up your writing and exactly when you should take a break. Maybe you need shorter or longer writing sessions; we can only find the right rhythm for you with accurate tracking.

A Little Gift

I am working on a spreadsheet that I will send to anyone who takes the free gift at the beginning of this book. I'll email you a download link to my template. I'm putting a spreadsheet together because I want to provide you with every tool that you need to achieve success.

Track the Writing Experience

We also want to track your actual writing experience. You are not a robot, and how you feel during each writing session is important data.

When I use a fitness program to track my progress, it tracks how long each exercise took, what I accomplished, and the calories burned. Then it asks me how hard the workout was. It asks for my subjective experience.

There is a reason that the best programs include both subjective and objective tracking. What good is writing fast if you hate it?

This is where your notes will be useful. Write down simple notes for yourself such as, "I was struggling here," or, "I felt like I was in the zone here." Notes can be very effective.

You can put these notes on your spreadsheet, or you can hand-write them in your notebook. Every hour when you write down how many words you wrote, write down your new word total and how you felt about that session and any other special notes. "I was struggling with this scene," or, "I was struggling writing dialogue," or, "I felt slower."

That's very valuable information.

Tracking Tools

There are some automated programs as well, and on my 20K page, I'll show you a bunch of the different options out there. I don't like to fill my books with product reviews and links because I want to focus on the core message. The tools I use change all the time, and it's much easier to update my website as my techniques change.

All the tools I mention, links to different templates I use, and loads of additional content are available at https://servenomaster.com/20k. You don't have to try and remember a bunch of links, just that one. I made some videos demonstrating the tools that I like, so you can see what the software looks like in action.

There is also an entire blog series where I track my progress and write about my progress creating this book. There are some cool pictures of my little slice of paradise as well.

Go Public

Another tracking method is to create a group on social media or start a blog and post your rolling word counts. Each post can start with a word count, and then you write a paragraph about that writing session. You might not want your page to be so public, but some people do better with this type of motivation.

You can even record videos if you want to give your hands a rest.

My first big success online was a blog. It was never meant to become public. It was a way of tracking my progress on a project and writing about my experiences. Back then I thought of a blog as a private diary online.

Anything that other people can see creates a sense of accountability. Your readers and followers will expect those regular updates. If you respond to accountability, this tracking method can be very useful.

Knowing what works for you is important. If you are terrified of sharing your word counts publicly, then there is no need to use this method.

Some of us respond to positive reinforcement, and some respond to negative reinforcement. Knowing your personality is critical. Be honest with yourself, and you can decide which tracking method works the best for you.

The number one most efficient way to increase your writing totals is to experiment with every aspect of this process, including how you track.

If using spreadsheets makes you more efficient, but you never fill them in, it's not the best process for you. Find a method that works for you and one that you can maintain.

This is the first step on the path to writing fast.

Marathon Writers

Our goal is to become marathon writers. We want to be able to write consistently over the span of days and weeks, not just for twenty minutes.

Words per day are our core metric, but it's not precise enough when you are in the development and training phase. We want to find at what point you enter the zone and then at what point you feel it fade away. While building up your skill set, we will use that words per hour metric.

When learning how to type, we track words per minute. Most people who transcribe or take notes for a living track words per minute. However, that is way too precise for the 20K process. It would make you less efficient.

Pomodoro Blocks

During some of your training exercises, you will write for specific blocks of time. When you do this, you need to track the number of words you write and how long each session is. As you master this sprinting technique, you may transition into a Pomodoro writer. This is where you write for a specific block of time and then take a break for a specific block of time and then get back to writing.

We will cover Pomodoro in much greater detail later in this book. When we start testing that technique you will need to write down the time you started a block, the length, how many words you wrote and how long your break was.

It is important that the way you track matches the way you are training and writing. Our goal is to generate numbers that we can use to adjust your writing process.

Stamina

Before we play around with Pomodoro blocks, you will start with sprinting sessions. With a sprint, you will write as much as you can in a fixed block of time. We will keep extending the length of that block until we find the limit of your stamina.

How many words can you write in how many minutes? This is the measure of stamina, and it will take a little while to get there.

Words Per Day

In addition to your precise words per hour or words per block tracking, you also need to track your words per day. This is the real number that will control your destiny as a writer. This figure measures the distance between you and the finish line for that book you're working on. It will tell you what you can commit to if a publisher comes and asks you to write a book of a certain length.

Writers at the top of their game know exactly how long a project will take them. They can estimate exactly how long each part of the writing process will take. The more accurate your timelines, the more you can charge for writing projects. You become a known quantity, and that higher level of trust will generate larger paychecks.

Most projects come with a word count and a deadline. It is much better to refuse a project than to take on more than you can handle and fail. Because I am a professional writer, I know my numbers.

I know I can easily write 10,000 words a day. Writing 20,000 words a day, however, is more serious and requires the majority of my focus. It will probably take me five to six hours of writing to hit that bigger number, but I can bang out 10,000 words in a few hours while maintaining my other projects.

I know my writing speed because I have made a living as a writer for years and I track my projects in great detail.

Endurance

Endurance is how many hours you can write each day. At a certain point, your mind or body becomes too exhausted to write anymore. You reach the edge of your endurance.

Normally endurance is a measure of how long you can write until you get distracted or fatigued. With dictation, I have to track how long I can speak before I notice problems in my throat. As soon as I feel any soreness developing, I have to stop each session.

When you're writing with your hands, pay attention to when you start feeling the first glimmers of fatigue. You don't want to push yourself too hard today and affect your performance tomorrow. If you write 20,000 words today, but tomorrow you are so worn out that you can only write 1,000, it's not worth it.

Pay close attention to your physical state. If your hands start to get tired or hurt, stop writing. Any issue with your body cannot be ignored. Write down any part of your body that hurts as part of your endurance tracking.

Spirit

Our final metric is the one that most writers ignore, yet it is critical. Keep a finger on your emotional pulse. Keep a record of your emotional state, any feelings of fatigue, and the overall quality of your work.

If you notice that your work has a lot more mistakes suddenly, you want to keep track of that. Just make a note of it for now. We don't need to worry about doing a lot of spellchecking and grammatical checks while writing, but we want to notice when our quality starts to decrease.

If you push yourself too far, you can alter your emotional state. If you are in a bad mood, tired or feeling out of sync, your writing will often reflect that. You don't want your emotional state to block you from writing that next crucial scene.

Writing Fast is not Writing Badly

Writing fast is not an excuse to write poorly. It's very important to maintain the quality of your work even as you improve your writing speed.

This is why we're going to track how long it takes to edit. If you double your writing speed but half your editing speed, you might come out a loser. We don't want that to happen because of a tracking error.

Writing is about project completion, and that is our ultimate measurement. We are looking for a net increase in your efficiency. I don't want to rob Peter to pay Paul. If writing and editing a book takes you sixty hours combined right now, that is your baseline. If writing faster causes you to make more mistakes, thus slowing down your editing process, you could end up spending seventy hours on the same project.

If that happens, you've gotten worse, not better. You must track your entire process to ensure you catch any glitches like this as quickly as possible.

External Variables

The main limitation on my writing speed is my fingers. The speed with which I can move my fingers and type controls how fast I can write. At a certain point in the day, my fingers begin making mistakes that my brain isn't making. There is a disconnect between my thoughts and my fingers. This is the first signal that I'm getting fatigued, and it's time to stop writing for the day. I have reached the limit of my endurance.

You can create just as much content as you do now in less time; it's your body and your physicality that is limiting you. Everything I'm going to teach you is going to increase how quickly you accomplish the same tasks.

The exercises and techniques in this book are designed to decrease the difference in how fast you think and how fast you write. The closer we can get to those two numbers, the closer we are to hitting your real maximum writing speed.

Once you begin tracking your different numbers, be sure to also track any new variable that changes. Some examples include:

- if you write in different locations
- if you write using different computers
- if you dictate some sections into the computer
- if you dictate other sections into your phone

Initially, you will want to limit these variables so that you can maximize your speed with a single baseline. Let's focus on maximizing your speed while writing on your computer at your current prime working location, before adding other variables.

If you cannot control your situation, then at least track any of these extra variables. You will start to notice that you write faster listening to different music or in a different location. Even a different seat in your favorite coffee shop can alter your speed. If you sit facing the street, you might be distracted by all the people walking by.

Someone else might be the opposite and write slower when facing a wall, as the blank wall starts to depress them.

Everyone is unique, and only experimentation will help us perfect your writing process. We are scientific partners on this venture, and I want you to hypothesize and think about changes you should make to improve your numbers.

You are the Driver

Track every variable when you write, and at the end of each week, examine what went right and what went wrong. Ask yourself what you can do next week to improve.

I'm giving you a set of skills and tools you can use to improve your writing speed. However, you are in the driver's seat. You must actively participate in this process. Look at what works for you and what doesn't work for you. Try new things and be proactive in this process. You are the only one who can track your progress and analyze your data to find ways to improve. The more you actively participate, the shorter the time between now and when you're a much faster writer.

Action Steps

1. You must come up with a system for tracking how many words you write each day. Decide if you will use a notebook, spreadsheet, word document or another method.

2. Use your tracking system. If you need to buy a special notebook, go do it right now.

3. Begin tracking your metrics immediately. How many words did you write yesterday?

4. Once a week, look at your records to help you figure out how, where, and when you are most productive.

5. Track your state of mind. Sometimes it's good to give up a little efficiency for more happiness.

6. Whenever you make a change in your writing, track it.

7. Achieving micro goals are critical to success, and Scrivener is a great way to track them.

8. Analyze your writing data to figure out when you should write and when you should take breaks.

THE ART OF RESEARCH

I am a story-teller, and I look to academic research... for ways of augmenting story-telling.
  - Malcolm Gladwell

Know Your Audience

Whether you're writing fiction or nonfiction, certain parts of your research process will be the same. However, they do diverge when you transition into the deep outlining phase. Telling a story is different from educating people.

Research starts with understanding what your audience wants. Many authors make the mistake of sitting down with an idea they want to write about and immediately cranking out a book. They publish it on Amazon, and when no one reads it, it's devastating.

The brilliance of Amazon is that every book is ranked. You can look at any book and see how many copies sold in the last day, the last week, and the last month.

Don't Invent the Wheel

Research begins by looking at the categories that are popular and the ones that relate to the subject you want to write about. Look in your desired category at the books that are doing well. Your book should be similar to these if you want financial success.

In whichever category you're going into, there are a few things you need to look at. Look at the type of book titles that exist in your space.

- How are the titles structured?
- Are there subtitles?
- How long are the books?

In some spaces, the book needs to be under 100 pages, and in other spaces it needs to be over 400. The rules and expectations are different for every category. They are not universal.

Give the People Bread and Circuses

There's a balance between what you want to write about and what people want to hear about, and the more you pay attention to that balance, the more you can achieve success. It's very hard to be successful writing about something that no one cares about or writing for a genre no one enjoys.

Build the Scaffolding

Research is about finding your audience, but it's also about:

- finding out what people enjoy
- how chapters are structured
- how long the books are
- what people like about those books
- what type of books do well

- what type of books don't do well

Be Your Best Customer

During your research process, you also want to look at forums and reviews to see what the audience is saying online.

People will post about what they liked and didn't like about books. "I loved this about the book, but I just wish this type of story-line would get written..."

Hearing what people want is valuable because you can create stories and get inspiration from their ideas.

When you write a book that meets someone's desires, you can message them directly to say they inspired you. You have a prebuilt fanbase that will write you raving reviews and spread the message for you.

Action Steps

1. Where can you find great book ideas?

2. What should you learn about a category before you start writing your book?

3. How can you be sure that an audience exists?

4. Why is it worth visiting forums and blogs on a topic?

FOUR THOUSAND WORDS
PER HOUR

One of the best pieces of advice I ever got was from a horse master. He told me to go slow to go fast. I think that applies to everything in life. We live as though there aren't enough hours in the day but if we do each thing calmly and carefully we will get it done quicker and with much less stress.
- Viggo Mortensen

Know What You're Writing

Know your plan. You want to have an outline that is as detailed as possible. The more detailed your outline is, the easier it will be for you to go through this process.

We want to break up your writing project into as many small tasks as possible. Writing will become easier for you when you plan, build a structure, and divide your process into small pieces. As writing becomes easier, the words flow more quickly.

When outlining, always go into as much detail as possible. The deeper you outline, the easier everything else is. A good outline removes majority of the stress that can come from writing. All these steps will make this process easier for you.

- Sit down and decide what you're going to write about.
- Decide how each scene is going to play out.
- Decide which facts you are going to go use for each section.

You have to do those other things. I know that is not the glamorous part of writing. And it's not even writing; it's research. Research is about decision-making.

Trying to mix decision-making with being creative always leads to failure. You are attempting to activate two different parts of your brain simultaneously, and that will always lower your daily word counts. This is the number one cause of writer's block.

Writing Rhythm

There are several different techniques for building and designing your writing rhythm. We want to start at the scientific end of the spectrum, and over time we will get more and more creative.

The Pomodoro technique is a very scientific method. It's very helpful for some writers, and I want to give you all the choices so that you can experiment.

At its most basic level, this process is about dividing your day up into blocks.

In some Pomodoro techniques, you write for twenty minutes and then you do something else. You break your day up into twenty-minute blocks, and you're not allowed to use more than two blocks in a row for any single task.

Dictate the Pain Away

We will endeavor to find the perfect writing blocks and break lengths for you. We are building a custom Pomodoro program from the ground up, rather than using a one-size-fits-all strategy.

Pomodoro was not designed for writers. It doesn't make sense to stop in the middle of a chapter when you are in the zone just because the timer goes off. There are two ways of writing, and we will use both of them to speed up your skill: writing for time and writing for topic.

When you are testing this technique, track how many words you write during each block. Then track how many blocks you can write per day. Pay attention to when you have faster and slower blocks. When you notice a pattern, adjust your writing strategy. If you write quicker in the morning, move more blocks into the morning.

Action Steps

1. Create a detailed outline before you start to write. The deeper you outline, the easier everything else. Decide what you are writing about, how each scene will play out, and which facts you will use in each section.

2. Divide every writing task into the smallest pieces possible.

3. Will you start by writing for time or content?

4. Experiment with yourself to see where you get the best results.

5. Commit to trying the 20K System until you find the perfect writing rhythm for you.

6. Try to mix other tasks and breaks into your workday to avoid fatigue.

WRITING A KILLER OUTLINE

The more work you put in on your outline and getting the skeleton of your story right, the easier the process is later.
- Drew Goddard

Plan to Succeed

The foundation for any writing project is preparation.
   You shorten the entire process when:

- you have your outline in place
- you have your notes in place
- you have everything properly organized
- you have all the references that you want to use prepared

   When you have everything organized before you start, your writing becomes unfettered. When you have to go back and look up things or try to remember what you want to do, you slow yourself down. When you have to enter different mental states, it slows down the writing process.

Before you start writing, you want to have the perfect outline in place. We want to have every piece of structure properly organized so that when we're writing, all we're doing is writing.

Outline the First Layer

With the 20K System, we outline in waves. With a mind map, each wave is one layer farther out. We end up with three or four layers of circles that are larger with each round of outlining.

The innermost circle is your table of contents, and that is where we will start. We begin with the big picture and work our way out, filling in each new layer with more detail.

I'm a big fan of mind mapping. All of my outlines are circular rather than linear. I change the chapter order of my books all the time. During my writing and editing process, I often discover that some sections need to move.

When you're building an outline, whether you're writing fiction or nonfiction, the story needs an arc. It needs a beginning and an end. This book is nonfiction, but there is still an emotional journey. You can feel that we've started somewhere and that we are on the path to a destination. There is a flow to the story.

A Delicious Layer Cake

Each of my books starts with a mind map built of three layers.

There's the inner layer, which is simply the titles of ten to fifteen chapters. The next layer is the structure of content within those chapters, which can be anywhere from three to twenty subsections that include the notes and the details that will go into each little section.

The final and outermost layer of my mind map comprises the bullet points I want each section to cover. When I convert my mind map to Scrivener, these bullet points will appear on the actual text section, and as I write, they get replaced.

The Lay of the Land

Developing a great outline starts with competitive research. Look at similar books in the genre. When I'm designing a nonfiction book, I read every other book I can find on a similar topic. I have read every book about writing fast, dictation, and the structure of a story to see how they are organized.

I also look at the reviews of these books. I want to see what people liked and didn't like about other similar books to be sure I include everything that those reviewers wanted to see. I also visit forums and blogs on the topic. I want to connect with what people need to hear and with what people need to know.

Every Story has a Rhythm

Every story must follow a series of beats in the correct order. The beats are the rhythm of the story; they are the timing and spacing of events within your story. Once we have our outline, which covers the journey, we want to think about the spacing of events.

Good Beginnings

The opening of any story is the most important part.

The first scene is the setup for the characters or the problem that the main character will face later. A bad first chapter can cause most of your readers to put down the book, and they will never discover that it gets better later.

I change, tweak, rewrite and reorder the first chapter of my book more than any other section. The first sentence is your biggest chance to draw the reader into your story and get them addicted to finding out how it ends.

Creating a Deep Outline

There is a phase in between the completion of the outline and your first rough draft which is often called a skeleton, sketch, pre-rough draft, or rough outline. In this phase, you turn your outline into more of a structure that's usable.

When developing the skeleton, I might write a few notes about the content that is going to be in each section.

I start with a few key notes, and I build on those to create my deep outline. As I add more detail and bullet points, this rough outline transitions into a full skeleton or deep sketch. When I'm writing the book, I want more than just section headings to work with. The bullet points I'm adding here become the waypoints that I travel through when I'm writing the book. The deeper your outline, the faster your writing phase will become.

It's easier to create a story by layers than it is to start at the beginning of your story and just create everything as you go. It is difficult to generate character development, story arcs, conflict, scenes, and an emotional journey all on the fly.

The more you prepare each different layer before you get to the writing phase, the easier and faster it will become, and the better your stories will be. People should be able to read your sketch and know if they like your story.

If there are any structural issues, it is much easier to correct them before you have written 100,000 words. If you wait until you've written the first draft, diagnosing and repairing problems is a nightmare.

The Rough Draft

Once your sketch is complete, it's time to begin the rough draft. Writing a rough draft is about free-form. Worrying about spelling mistakes, grammar mistakes, and little errors will slow you down.

Keep your editing and writing phases separate. We want to break your writing process into three distinct phases. We have completed the outlining phase and are beginning the writing phase. The editing and correction phase comes later, so don't worry about that now.

If you skip over deep outlining, creating beats, or working on your sketch to get right to the rough draft, it's only going to slow you down and leave holes in your story development. We write in this order to make the process faster and more efficient.

If you've hit writer's block, written thousands of words that you're unhappy with, or if you struggle to finish a book, it always comes down to lack of preparation and outlining.

Little Things Add Up

More than anything else, at this point in the book, I want you to remember that fast and efficient writing is about chopping each task into small, manageable tasks. The more small sections you break your outline into, the easier it is to write faster and the better the quality of your work will be. If you organize your story into large sections, it's challenging to write quickly.

The three phases of writing your book are:

1. Prepare
2. Write
3. Edit

Phase One is researching, outlining, and sketching. Phase Two is the writing process. Here is where you create your first version and your big rough draft. Phase Three is the rewriting and editing phase. The more efficient and more successful you are in Phase One, the shorter the other two phases become.

If you run into that moment where you notice your word counts are consistently low and you're struggling, the problem is in your outlining, research, and preparation process.

When you hit a wall or get stuck, just put your pencil down. Go and do another task and come back later. You could even work on another section of the book. There is no rule that says a book must be written in the order in which it is read.

You're allowed to change the order of your sections. As long as the final product of the book is good, the way you created it is irrelevant.

Action Steps

1. Perform some competitive research: other authors' table of contents, and reader reviews.

2. Find a book that you want to model. Break down the beats, write them down, and use that to start your outline.

3. Write a detailed sketch or skeleton of your whole book.

4. Write your rough draft - no editing allowed yet. This is the part where you just let your creative juices flow.

5. Diligently track your word counts during the rough draft phase. Analyze your results carefully. The more data you have, the more useful it will be to you.

THE ZONE

As for the zone, I always find the zone immediately after I am sure I will never ever find the zone again because it has left me for some other, better writer.
   - Sarah MacLean

The Runner's High

We've all been there and felt that moment where time just seems to disappear; you're writing so fast that you don't even feel the time flying by. You look at the clock and one or two hours have disappeared.

This is the perfect state of writing nirvana. We want to achieve this state as quickly as possible. Once we are in the zone, we have achieved the perfect state of concentration. When all distractions disappear, writing goes from difficult to easy.

Our goal in this section is to diagnose and discover exactly how to get you into the zone and turn this from guesswork into a replicable process. To become a fast writer, we need to reach this state as frequently and as quickly as possible.

You don't need additional techniques and tools to find the zone. Often, it's about minimizing distractions or removing the things that hold us back. It's hard to get in the zone when you're flipping back and forth between your document and a news website, YouTube, or your social media site.

We have distractions because we don't like to be bored. With the distractions that surround us, it is tempting to write a little bit, relax a little bit, and then write a little bit again. The problem with this process is that it keeps you from ever achieving the zone. It permanently keeps you out of the zone.

While having a nice distraction provides short-term pleasure, in the long-term it hurts you and decreases your effectiveness as a writer.

Declutter Your Mind

The first step in achieving the zone is removing external and internal distractions. If you have something in your life that you can't stop thinking about, it will block the zone just as much as the television.

We need to develop a way for you to clear your mind. You can try yoga or meditation to find your inner peace. We are all unique, so we will each need a different technique to relax.

One way to remove external or internal distractions is to handle all of your other decisions first before you begin writing.

People are Distracting

We need our minds calm and decluttered to achieve that perfect writing state.

A big challenge that you'll face is that other people don't take work at home seriously. If they see you at home on your computer, they think you're playing a game even if you're working on a project that will pay you $10 or $20 million. They don't realize that what you're doing is real work, not a hobby.

When people are most familiar with traditional employment, it can be difficult for them to understand that your income comes from you being on your computer. Most people can't connect with the idea of doing something that you like and getting paid for it. That sounds too unrealistic to them.

Train Your Friends

You must train the people around you to let you work. If not, they will constantly be distracting you and it will be impossible to achieve the zone. You must put systems in place that they can understand and know when it's zone time. This is work time; this is not playtime. One of the easiest ways to do this is by repetition. Do the same things consistently so those around you will learn.

You can train your body to know that it's zone time if you always sit in the same chair and work in the same location. Repetition of location and action is how we train ourselves. When your writing pattern is always different, you will struggle to find the zone. If you write at a different time every day, or if you write at different locations every day, the zone will remain elusive.

Ritual

There are other things that you can do to speed up your writing process. If you want to eliminate distractions, the first thing you need to do is turn off the internet. There's no reason to be online while you're writing. If you must do more research while you're writing, that is a sign that you haven't properly prepared for your writing sessions. All your research, and notes should be together in an offline format so that you can write without needing to be online.

We also need to firmly establish the rhythm of your day. You should always do daily activities such as eating, sleeping, and working consistently and at the same time each day.

"Write drunk, edit sober"

There are certain things that you should simply not do. I don't recommend drinking while writing. As much as it's fun, it becomes a distraction. On top of slowing down motor function as the alcohol floods into your system, it will also actively block you from getting into the zone.

We need to maintain a consistent state to remain in the zone and to write quickly. Playing a video game, watching a television show, talking to someone on the phone, and texting your friends are all distractions we need to eliminate.

Take the batteries out of the TV remote. Hide the video game controllers. Turn off your phone and put it in a drawer. Remove distractions before you begin, and your effectiveness will skyrocket. You will be shocked at how fast you can write without all that noise around you.

Skills and Talents

A large percentage of the population does not understand the difference between a skill and a talent.

A talent is something you're born with, and we're all born with a different mix of talents. We are strong and weak in different areas, but writing is not a talent; writing is a skill. It is something you can learn to develop and improve.

When you understand that writing fast is a skill, the easier this process will become. This idea that some people are born good at writing is just a false limitation. This belief will do nothing but slow you down.

Writing is a skill that you can develop and grow. Soon you'll easily be writing 20,000 words a day.

Put Your Sneakers On

Just like anything in life, to be able to write fast, you must train. Sprinting is one of the best ways to start strengthening your speed-writing muscles. Train yourself to write for a certain block of time while you push yourself as hard as you can. As you push yourself through these drills, you will discover that you can only maintain your focus for a certain amount of time. Everyone has a different amount of focus.

We don't know your available focus yet. We need to assess your current level. At this point, you have a plan, a writing location, you know how to remove distractions, the preparation is complete, and now it is time to write.

The First Sprint

Get to your primary writing location. It's time to start training yourself to maintain focus for longer. I want you to do a sprint-writing assessment.

Start with an outline for something you want to write. Upload it into Scrivener or whichever word processor you prefer. Turn off the Internet and all other distractions. Start a timer and write for as long as you can, as fast as you can.

It doesn't matter how long you last. Everyone will be different. This is a personal assessment. Whatever your initial block of time is, keep a record. This is our initial diagnostic to get a feel for your skill level.

Your sprint results today are a baseline that we can improve. And believe me, we are going to blow that first number right out of the water!

Writing Blocks

We want to train you to the point where you can do sprints of twenty or twenty-five minutes and then turn those into Pomodoro blocks. We can then build out sprint blocks throughout your day, and eventually you will develop the skill of marathon writing, which is where you can write for two- or three-hour blocks.

When we finish the drills and exercises in this book, we will find the best strategy for you. Whether it's writing for a long time with a longer break or writing for a shorter time and having a short break, all of these techniques are fine. Our goal is only to hit our word count at the end of the day.

Life is Full of Surprises

We're going to find the perfect pattern for you. For your first sprint, eliminate all distractions and try to replicate your natural writing conditions as much as possible. Use the location where you will do the majority of your writing. Measure how many words you write and how long your focus lasts. Make a note of anything else that affects your sprint. What was your first distraction? Did your phone ring or did your mind just start to wander? Did you start to get an itch in your back? For now, just make a note of what causes your focus to break.

If there is a particular thought that keeps popping into your mind, write that down as well. Sometimes we feel this immense pressure to complete a writing project, and that becomes the distraction. If there is a thought that you can't control, keep track of how often if affects your work. Self-assessment is about finding the most common distractions. Once we isolate them, we can deal with them.

STOP

Please stop reading right now and perform your first sprint. This is an interactive training, and the only way for the 20K System to work is if you put in the work. Go to your usual writing location and write as fast as you can until you get distracted. Start a timer and write for as long as you can. When you lose focus or become distracted, stop the timer. After you finish this first sprint, go to the next section to analyze your results.

Results

Now that you've completed your first sprint, we want to do an analysis. Keep a permanent record of your sprints, starting with this one. Your focus, for now, is NOT on the quality of your words or grammar. We will deal with that separately.

Instead, you just want to focus on writing as many words as possible. If during your sprint you caught yourself going back and re-editing words or changing grammar or fixing spelling, we have isolated our first opportunity. Those little edits are all slowing down your word count.

The more we can handle those types of errors in the editing phase, the better. The editing phase engages the logical part of your mind, whereas the writing process is very creative. Our writing process starts out analytical, as we research and prepare our notes and outlines. We then enter the creative phase, where we write as quickly as we can. The final phase again engages your analytical and logical mind as you edit your work.

Bringing the logical part of your brain into the writing process will only slow you down. You can fix your misspellings later just as well. You might feel that itch in the back of your mind that requires fixing these errors on the fly, but you need to overcome that.

Turn off all the spell and grammar checks in your word processor. Eliminate or deactivate any other alerts or distractions you discovered during your first sprint.

Write down your first sprint results: how long it lasted, how many words you wrote, what distracted you, what was good and what was bad. Self-analysis is very beneficial at this point.

This will help you as you move forward because you now have a baseline, your first sprint. One of the advantages of writing in blocks or with a very specific goal in front of you is that you will begin to feel what it's like to complete projects.

Each time you finish a little project, no matter how small, you get a feeling of accomplishment and success.

The more feelings of accomplishment we can generate in the process of writing, the more likely you are to complete the process. We're trying to develop along this path a strong set of positive affirmations. Rather than feeling down every time you fail to hit a goal or fail to complete your book, we want to replace those negative emotions with positive emotions.

Positive reinforcement of these tiny steps is the key to habit change. You should be proud of yourself right now for completing your first writing sprint. You've done something new, and you're developing a new skill.

Later we will discover together how to refine the editing process, even when you have more errors than usual.

I have some helpful techniques in the editing process that will help you edit quickly. You don't have to worry about editing for right now. Separate the creative and logical parts of the writing process, and each individual part will be much faster.

Words Per Hour

With your first sprint completed, we can assess how quickly you write, what your true speed is, what your true ability is. This is not a typing program, so we're not tracking words per minute. That's too small. The number we want to see is words per hour, so we have to do a little math here and figure out how many words you can write per hour. If you just wrote for three minutes, take the number of words you wrote, multiply that by twenty and that gives us your words per hour.

If you wrote for a more difficult amount of time, we'll need to apply more difficult math. Take the number of words you wrote, divide that by how many minutes you wrote for and then multiple this number by sixty.

$$\frac{WordsYouWrote x 60}{MinutesYouWrote} = WordsPerHour$$

This is a rough estimate of how many words you would write in a one-hour sprint.

Words per hour is the first metric we're going to work on improving together. It is not the final metric, and it is not the most important metric. Focusing on words per hour is good if you're focused on writing blog posts or newspaper articles. If you want to write much larger projects, then knowing how many words you can generate per day is more important.

Action Steps

1. Eliminate as many distractions as possible.

2. Commit to breaking through the initial writing phase and hitting the zone.

3. Train the people around you to respect your writing zone.

4. Develop a writing ritual and take it very seriously.

5. Believe that writing is a skill and that makes it possible to improve.

6. Do a sprint session to find a benchmark of words per hour. Track what caused you to lose focus.

7. Keep tracking your words per hour and words per day.

8. Keep notes about all of the distractions that kick you out of your zone and the things that interfere with you even getting into your zone at all.

THE ART OF
EXPERIMENTATION

There are three principal means of acquiring knowledge... observation of nature, reflection, and experimentation. Observation collects facts; reflection combines them; experimentation verifies the result of that combination.
    - Denis Diderot

Trained to Distract Ourselves

Distractions are one of the biggest challenges for this career. Any career where you're the boss, or the entrepreneur, requires a great deal of focus.

When you're working for yourself, efficiency is far more important. If we can create a day where you can work for eight hours without any distractions, we will quadruple your productivity. You will get a week's worth of writing done every single day.

Email is so Distracting

To overcome time-wasting distractions, we must build systems. I use a very simple system to prevent losing six hours a day to email; I only check my email once a day. By having a fixed time to check email, I no longer feel any urgency to check email again the rest of the day. I used to be a smartphone guy who had my phone connected to over a dozen different email accounts.

The key to transitioning to one email check a day is managing expectations. I tell everyone that I only check my email once a day. It's one of the first things I tell new contacts. When they expect it, they no longer overreact when it takes me a day to reply to them. My coaching clients all know that I check my email every evening between six and eight P.M. EST.

By implementing this system, I have more freedom and less stress in my life.

The Skill of Focus

We are trying to develop the skill of focus. Our skills can always be improved, and the skill of focus is no different.

I don't have the attention span to work on the same book for months on end. Some authors spend months or even years writing their book, but that doesn't work for me. So I've developed a system that allows me to write very quickly.

When you're dealing with distraction, when you're dealing with your focus issues (and you will have them because everyone does), it's vital to self-analyze. We're going to test different techniques to see which one works best for you.

The Great Pomodoro Experiment

There is no universal technique for writing fast that works for everyone.

Because I've worked with so many authors, I know that everyone writes in different ways. Everyone needs different techniques because we're all different and unique. Some people learn visually, some learn through sound, and some learn from writing. We all learn in different ways, and we know that there's tons of science behind that; this process is the same thing.

The only way to find your numbers is through experimentation and testing. This is a process where we can get better results by having a solid testing strategy.

You are a Snowflake

Rather than just giving everyone a single process that doesn't work for many people, we now have a system that you can develop and improve yourself. You can continually become a better writer.

It is time to start studying yourself as we enter a phase of experimentation. Try writing at different times of the day. Experiment with different types of sprints. Mix up the lengths of your sprints and the breaks you take in between them. Track yourself writing dialogue versus writing action scenes versus writing exposition.

Each writing process is a little bit different, and the more you can self-analyze without attaching negative emotions to the process, the better your writing will become. When you try twenty-five-minute Pomodoro writing sessions with five-minute breaks, and they don't work, do NOT call that a failure. Focus on the fact that you have eliminated another possible technique from your list. You are one step closer to success.

When you hit a setback, I want you to say, "That's not the right technique for me. I will continue to experiment, and I'm going to find the method that works for me best." The 20K System is a process. Becoming a fast and efficient writer is a process, not a single moment.

Hold the Breaks

I have been a professional writer for seven years, and I'm still finding ways to improve my writing skills. My quality is certainly better now than when I started. I'm always looking for ways to improve my process.

When you are experimenting with different writing blocks, you must be very strict with the length of your breaks. Measuring your breaks is critical. If you choose to spend your break on Facebook or watching television, it is very easy to lose track of time.

If you're in the middle of reading a newspaper article and your timer beeps, you need to switch gears immediately. One of the reasons I prefer longer writing sessions is that I also prefer longer breaks.

If you are in the middle of a distraction and the alarm beeps, it can take you longer to get back into the writing rhythm. It takes me five to ten minutes to get back into my writing groove. For those first few minutes, I still have leftover thoughts swirling in my brain. If I only wrote for ten-minute sessions, I would never even get close to the zone.

Don't start anything that will take longer than the length of your break. It can mess up your timing and ruin your tracking results.

Broken Rhythm

You need a beginning and an end to whatever you choose to do during your break time.

The danger when you're developing your new writing rhythm is that if you extend your breaks you lose your rhythm. It will affect everything else. You might have a great twenty-minute sprint, but then if you extend your five-minute break into ten minutes, your entire schedule will be knocked off course.

Experiment with yourself. The more you learn about yourself, the easier this entire process will become.

Action Steps

1. Make a plan to eliminate your most common distractions.

2. Turn non-priority tasks, such as reading the news or checking your email, into once-a-day tasks.

3. Track your breaks as well as your writing sprints.

4. Test longer and shorter breaks and pay attention to how your break length affects your word counts and ability to get into the zone.

5. Find break activities that match your break lengths.

ADVICE IS WORTH
THE PRICE

The only thing to do with good advice is to pass it on. It is never of any use to oneself.
   - Oscar Wilde

I am a Writer

There are as many opinions as there are people in the world. Everyone likes to give writing advice. Everyone acts like an expert, but getting advice from someone who is not a writer is very dangerous.

Once you find a method that works for you, test and improve it, but don't listen to someone else about what works for them.

Before I take someone's advice, I always check their credibility. If someone offers me a piece of advice and they've never finished a book, I know that piece of advice is garbage.

Choose your Destination

You should only take advice from people who are living a life that you want to replicate. If you want to live on a tropical island and dictate your books while sitting on a beautiful beach in paradise, then my advice might be worth following. I've worked very hard to get where I am. If you follow what I do, you'll end up with the same result.

Get advice from people you want to replicate.

The person you take advice from is your destination. If you take advice from someone who has a life that you don't want, then you'll end up with a life you don't want Right now you're in a process where you're trying to learn things. You should only follow the 20K system if my approach to writing and life appeal to you.

Protecting Your Success

I don't like to change things, but people want to give me advice all the time. There's nothing worse than unsolicited advice. I never give people writing advice unless they ask for it.

As someone who's worked in the advice and coaching field for a long time, I know this lesson well. I don't give people advice without them asking. I don't tell anyone about how to write faster or how to become a great writer unless they ask me.

When you tell people that you are learning to write faster, they will see an opportunity to offer you advice, and I don't want someone else to mess up what we are doing together.

Luck is Never a Factor

Your writing process will be different than mine and every other reader of this book. Everyone writes in a different way. I want you to find the way that works best for you through experimentation. The only effective method to becoming a massive speed writer is self-experimentation; no other method works.

Master One System

If you start Karate, Tae Kwon Do, and kickboxing classes at the same time, you will struggle to succeed. You will learn different methods, and the messages will get confusing. In Tae Kwon Do you kick with your foot, but in kickboxing you kick with your shin. Use the wrong technique in the wrong class, and you could end up hurting someone or breaking the bones in your foot.

I don't want you to break your writing foot!

If you study just one martial art, you learn how to fight. If you try to learn them all the same time, you'll just be confused. They all have different systems. Each of their systems works, but when you mingle them all together before you're ready, you'll achieve no success.

Stick to one system until you achieve some success and then add on new techniques. That's how you will become a master writer.

If you want to add techniques from another system, wait until after you have mastered the 20K System.

Action Steps

1. Trust but Verify. Never take advice from someone who doesn't have the life and experience you want.

2. Don't try to learn multiple writing systems at the same time. Many systems work, but not when you mingle steps from different paths.

3. Be prepared for unsolicited advice from people around you and have a plan for how to deal with it.

4. Lock down your real goal for reading this book. Do you want to

write fast just to impress other people? Do you want to write fast to make more money? Write down your goal somewhere you can see it every day.

5. Do everything in your power to remove luck as a factor in your success.

INCREASE YOUR SPEED

Just remember, once you're over the hill you begin to pick up speed.
   - Arthur Schopenhauer

Write Faster

There are some simple tweaks that will help you to write much faster very quickly. These small tweaks will increase your results with your writing sprints. There are some limitations and distractions that nearly every writer has to deal with at some point in their career.

The first hurdle is your hands. The faster you type, the faster you write. Unfortunately, many of us never studied typing in school, either because we are too old or too young. Most of us picked up our typing skills through playing around on the computer.

Learn to Type

Start with a touch typing program. Touch typing is when you type without looking at the keys. If you ever have to take a peek down to find where a key is, then you need to start with one of these programs. No matter where you are in your writing career, you should take a typing speed assessment today. There is a link on the 20K page to my favorite assessment tool.

How fast you can type is controlled by how fast your hands can operate. Your hand speed will affect how fast everything else in this process works.

The faster you type, the faster everything else will work. Completing writing projects faster will dramatically affect your life. Typing is the foundation skill upon which the skill of writing is built.

Control your Computer

Remove distractions from inside your word processor. We've already looked at some external distractions, but now it's time to look inside your actual tool.

Word processors like to be helpful and notify you every time you make a mistake. They like to draw your attention to every error while you're writing. This is a fairly new invention. Word processors have not always pointed out your mistakes without you checking for them.

When computers were first created, they didn't have the processing power to scan for errors while you were writing. This supposed improvement has slowed down most writers. It makes life more inefficient for professional writers. Your computer can process on the fly and will gladly highlight every mistake you make and underline it in red. This is incredibly distracting. Ignoring red ink on the page is hard.

As you're writing, you see all these red mistakes and are tempted to go back and fix them. This will slow you down. Editing and correcting on the fly, unfortunately, mingles the creative process with the analytical process of editing. Turn your spellcheck off. All you do is uncheck one little box and so much stress disappears. Turn off your grammar check and any other alerts as well. You can turn them back on when you are editing, but not during the creative process.

Your goal is to create as many words as you can, as fast as you can.

Don't use your backspace key and don't do any destructive editing. It's tempting, but it takes up valuable time.

Unhelpful Friends

Another dangerous distraction is the "helpful" friend. If you have someone who wants to read each chapter as soon as it is finished, that will affect your entire writing process.

If you have people that want to read something as soon as you write it, you need to shut them down. When I launch a book and wait for that first round of feedback, I'm always on pins and needles. You have created something, and you want people to like it. Letting someone read your book while you are writing will leave you in this state perpetually.

You don't want to lock yourself into this state during the creative process. There is no way you'll feel comfortable showing someone a draft that you know is loaded up with spelling mistakes. So you'll turn spellcheck on, and now your helpful friend has slowed you down in two different ways.

Anything that slows down your writing flow or messes with your focus needs to be eliminated.

Unexpected Surprises

I prefer to use different locations for work and play. The more you repeat behavior, the easier it is for people to memorize it. If you are always working in different places, it will take people longer to recognize when you are working and when it's a good time to talk to you.

Once people learn your rhythm, things get a lot easier. You might go through a small period of trial and error, but repetition and consistency is how others will learn your patterns.

Action Steps

1. Take the touch typing assessment at ServeNoMaster.com/20K

2. Improve your typing by investing in typing software and practice.

3. Turn off distractions (spellcheck/grammar check/etc.) from the word processor you are using.

4. Try different work patterns until you figure out what works for you. Test locations, times of day, and listening to music.

5. Train the people at each location to recognize when it's work time.

6. Consider finding a distant location to get away from the people who want to "help" you.

EXERCISES

For me, writing is an experience. It's an exercise in which I want to discover myself by taking my characters to the edges of human experience, to the edges of themselves and then, asking certain questions - about love, what does it mean to love? What's beauty? What is true beauty?
  - Ted Dekker

Time to Sweat

We have covered the big picture, and we have the framework for writing fast in place. Now it's time to put boots on the ground. In this section, we have a series of exercises that you can use to increase your writing speed.

There are a few key causes of slow writing. We need to isolate the cause of your slow writing and attack it directly. The causes of slower writing can be:

- Slow typing
- Slow writing

- Writer's block
- Analysis Paralysis

When your problem is the speed at which you type, no creative writing exercise will make a difference. The problem is mechanical, and we can attack it directly. For most people, this is the first and biggest challenge. We don't even realize that our hands are limiting our writing speed.

The problem can be that you write slowly. You take time formulating each sentence in your mind and releasing it onto the page. There is a problem between getting the words out of your brain, through your body, and onto the page.

Writer's block is a common name for a group of different problems. Often it's caused by a lack of preparation in the outlining and research phase, but sometimes you're just stuck. You know what you want to happen in the scene, but the words won't flow. This is a creativity problem.

Finally, we have a group of fear-based problems that as a group cause paralysis by analysis. This manifests itself as going back and fixing every grammatical and spelling mistake before the editing phase. Or perhaps you keep deleting and rewriting scenes or balling up the page and throwing it into the trashcan. You end up rewriting the same scene over and over again.

The solution to each problem isn't always an exercise, but it certainly helps to have one available. We've already covered a few solutions to each of these problems, but now it's time for exercises that will help you break through before the problem occurs.

A Note About Tracking

You absolutely must track your numbers for these exercises to work. The more data points you track, the faster you will master the 20K System. Keep track of your performance over time as well. If you have a fantastic Monday but are too burned out to write a single word Tuesday, that needs to be in your notebook.

The last thing we want is to build a strategy around a false positive. It's not about writing as many words in a day as you can once; this system is about creating something replicable on a daily basis. By the time you complete your training, you will be able to write 20,000 words a day consistently. As a master of the 20K System, you will be able to generate 100,000 words per week and still enjoy a lovely long weekend.

Nothing is more important than tracking your numbers. Please don't slack off here or the system will falter.

Typing Drills

If your limitation is technical, then your first stop will be typing drills. If you have to look at your hands while you type, that will always slow you down. There are many free typing programs out there, and I have provided links to some of my favorites on the 20K page.

Even if you are pretty good at typing, I recommend taking the assessment and then playing with a few typing programs. Even if you only increase your typing speed by one word per minute, this adds up to sixty words per hour and over the course of a year can easily add up to an additional book for your catalog.

Small Sprints

Writing fast is a skill, and if you don't practice with enough frequency, it can atrophy. A small sprint is a way to keep up your skills even when life has you too busy for a proper writing session.

Every day, set aside five minutes to blaze through a little sprint. Write as much as you can in this tiny block. Keep track in your notebook and watch your numbers improve, even when you're busy with life.

There are a few critical rules for sprints that you must stick to. Turn off all spell and grammar checkers. Turn off all distractions. Do not hit delete or backspace no matter what happens. You are only focused on quantity, not quality. Do not allow the editing part of your mind distract you.

Your goal with small sprints is to grow. Start with five minutes and add a minute to your sprints every day. Keep track of your total word count and also your words per minute. You want to find the peak of your performance bell curve. Your best length may be nine minutes, or it may be twenty-seven minutes.

Once you have found your sprinting "sweet spot," you can move onto our Pomodoro exercises, which is a way of daisy-chaining small sprints.

Chain Your Sprints

We have talked about Pomodoro at a few points in this book, but let's dial into Pomodoro for writers. If you only dedicate forty minutes a day to writing, your book will take months to finish, no matter how fast you write. Therefore, we can't follow the traditional and strict Pomodoro guidelines.

Once you have found your small sprint "sweet spot" it's time to play with breaks. For some writers, short breaks are perfect. Other writers need longer breaks to find the zone. Consistent tracking of your word counts is critical here. It's the only way to find your peak writing rhythm.

For your first exercise, start with a one-hour block. Break it up into sprints and breaks. Track your performance with multiple sprints and play with longer and shorter breaks. If your break is too short, your mind won't feel rested. If it's too long, you will lose your rhythm and have to start over. You will lose your connection to the zone.

As you start to get in touch with your ideal rhythm, lengthen your writing block. Expand your session up to two hours and watch your word counts soar. Once you can handle a four-hour block of writing and controlled breaks, add in a longer break. I don't recommend writing for more than four hours without a long break because you risk burning out over the course of a few days. Don't forget that you need to write tomorrow as well.

Pushing yourself too hard today can cost you tomorrow, and that will hurt you in the long run.

Big Sprints

At a certain point, small sprints turn into big sprints, and eventually they turn into marathons. There is no official definition for these writing lengths, but according to my opinion, a small sprint is anything under thirty minutes, a big sprint is from thirty to ninety minutes, and a marathon is anything longer than ninety minutes. These numbers can be adjusted, but this is a good point of reference.

Some people are Pomodoro writers, and some are marathon writers. The only way to be sure is to test both methods and track your numbers fastidiously.

Big sprints are where we will keep pushing your writing speed and strengthen those mental muscles. Start off with sprint lengths that you can manage. You may start out at five minutes, but every few days add a minute to your timer. We want to push you past thirty minutes to see if you enter the zone. For many writers, there is a dip in performance right before they break into the zone and the numbers skyrocket again.

During a writing sprint, you must not stop writing. If you get stuck or run out of ideas, keep pushing yourself, and skip to another section of your book if you have to. After the sprint, you can go back and work on that section of your outline.

As always, keep track of your sprint times and word counts.

With the small sprint exercises, we found your wall. Now it's time to break through that wall and push until we find your true wall. We are training for a marathon here, and that means pushing yourself to the limit. When you can write for two hours straight, hitting ten or 20,000 words a day is a breeze.

After you have conquered your big sprint training, it's time to make some final decisions. Compare your performance with

Pomodoro blocks. Do you write more in two hours with blocks or a marathon? Which technique gives you more words per day?

Transcription Loop

This technique will help you to overcome a problem that may be hiding behind your "writer's block." Have you ever been trying to think of a certain word and it just won't come? You can feel it on the tip of your tongue, but you can't get the word to come out?

For many people, this is what writer's block feels like. The problem may not be that you don't know what is supposed to happen, but that you don't know how to say it. You can't seem to find the words you want to use to express yourself.

This is a technique that will help you to become a better writer. It's very similar to a method that I use to teach new copywriters how to master their craft.

Find a great book and get a paperback copy. Sit down every day and spend twenty to thirty minutes copying the book by hand.

Writing with a pen is a skill that we seem to lose after we graduate from school. When you write this way, you activate a different part of your brain and almost as if by magic, these powerful writing skills will be absorbed into your mind.

If you stick to this simple exercise, you will become an incredible writer in less than six months. I know that might seem like a long time, but even after a few weeks, you will notice that the words start to flow much easier.

Blind Writing

This is a simple ten-minute exercise that forces you to disconnect writing from editing. If you struggle to try and correct every misspelling while you are writing, this exercise will help you to break through. This technique comes with three rules.

1. Eyes closed

2. Write fast

3. Pen and paper

These rules will help you to push your writing to new heights. Without being able to see the page, you have no chance to go back and edit. If you try this with a keyboard, there is still the temptation to hit that delete key. With a pen, there is no delete key. Write as fast as you can during this exercise.

You can try this exercise with random topics, but I find that leaves room for writer's block to creep back in. I don't want you wasting time trying to come up with a new topic to write about every day. Instead, take a scene or section from your book and write it this way. This way of writing is crazy, but you will come up with some real nuggets of gold.

Look back at your page and circle your favorite words or sentences. Pick one and write it at the top of the next page in your notebook. Now do another ten-minute writing session with your eyes closed. You will be amazed at what you come up with.

This is an excellent way to warm up for a writing day as well.

Action Steps

1. Work your way through each of these drills and exercises.

2. Invest three weeks into improving your writing speed.

3. Track your numbers carefully in a notebook or spreadsheet.

4. Find a great book to copy by hand for your transcription exercises.

5. Commit to pushing through your writing walls to find how far you really can go with a big sprint.

SPEED TRAINING

Excellence is an art won by training and habituation. We do not act rightly because we have virtue or excellence, but we rather have those because we have acted rightly. We are what we repeatedly do. Excellence, then, is not an act but a habit.
  - Aristotle

Create a Plan

To succeed at anything in life, you need a plan. Even if you are only planning a few days into the future, this action will bring you closer to success.

For every book I write, I start with my goals. I know exactly how many words I want in the finished product. Whether you are writing blog posts, emails, sales letters, scripts, novels, or manuals, you must start out knowing your word count goal.

Planning is a critical component of any project. Here we have a different project. The goal is to write faster, and we need to plan out a long-term strategy to get there. Your plan should include the exercises from the previous section. Only you know how much time you have available. You may only have time for a small sprint every weekday and can work on your bigger sprints on the weekend.

Use a Calendar

Build out a calendar that has a strict schedule. Add a minute to your sprints at least once a week. If you can grow faster, do that. Start out with a daily calendar of when you will perform each exercise. From there you can build out a plan for the next week.

Only after you have tried each exercise a few times will you know which ones are right for you. After a week or two, you can build out a training plan that lasts an entire month.

If you can dedicate the full twenty-one days to the 20K System, you will see the fastest results. I understand that some people don't have that kind of time available, so creating a long-term calendar to slowly improve your writing is a very effective method.

Be Firm with Yourself

I could include a training calendar with this book, but it would be useless to 90 percent of the people who use it. I don't know what time you get up in the morning or which exercise you need to perform the most. You are in charge of your destiny. I have given you the tools to become an amazing writer; your job is to implement them.

Be strict with yourself. Reward yourself for doing all your drills and punish yourself for failure. This is like any other training regime; your destiny is in your hands. Treat this seriously and you can quite easily become a six-figure writer this year.

Training Versus Working

Set aside time each day that is purely for improving your writing. This time is separate from your work time. Even if you only dedicate thirty minutes a day to training, you will keep growing as a writer and your writing speed will improve.

Finding the correct balance can be a challenge at first, but set a clear goal right now. How many words do you want to write per hour? Per day? Per week?

Keep separate training sessions until you blast through all three of your initial goals. Until you can write 20,000 a day consistently, maintain your training sessions.

Action Steps

1. Start every project with a clear word count target.

2. Plan when you are going to do these exercises and put them on a calendar.

3. Commit to twenty-one days to master the 20K System.

4. Continue your exercises and drills until you can hit 20,000 words a day consistently.

5. Find some client work and get paid while you learn.

THE 20K HABIT

Winning is habit. Unfortunately, so is losing.
  - Vince Lombardi

The Two Failures

I want to give you a strong basic understanding of habits and some of the exciting stuff that's going to be coming out in my next book. I want to give you enough to implement immediately so you don't have to wait for my next book. You can become a fast, successful writer with great habits right here!

Habit all comes down to how our brains process information. Our brains are designed to find effective strategies to help us get the results we want. When we try something and get a bad result, our brain starts to learn from that. And it usually works.

There is a big difference between **systemic failure** and **random failure**. Please pause for a moment and memorize those two terms. If you have ever hit a wall or felt like a failure, this lesson will change your life.

Most of us mix up these two types of failures.

Systemic failure is when the same failure happens over and over again, but we don't change our behavior. Think of the mouse that keeps getting shocked trying to get the same piece of cheese.

Random failure is where each failure happens at a different point in the process. The mouse walks into a trap in one part of the maze; then it gets lost, then it falls into the water. Each of these failures is different.

Blame the Universe

Unfortunately, we often run into random failure and think that it's systemic. This misdiagnosis leads us to blame the universe for our troubles.

When you blame one of these third-party factors, you give away your power. The more you blame one of these external forces, the less chance you have to turn things around and improve your life.

Systemic Failures are Easy to Fix

If you've been trying to write a book for two years, and you haven't written a single word, then you have a systemic problem. The unwritten book is a systemic problem, but there is a good chance that if we dig deeper, we can find a series of distractions that knocked you off course.

Isolate the Problem

There are two steps to finding and conquering any systemic failure. The first is to clearly define your goal. If you don't have a clearly defined goal, don't be surprised if you never hit it.

The second step is to isolate the cause of the problem.

If you have a long-term project that never gets finished, you can look at all of your attempts to work and try to find the cause. If you're anything like me, each time you started on the project something new distracted you. All of these little failures knocked you off course. The big picture is that you don't have enough focus.

At first, it sounds like a systemic failure. The reality is that each of these little failures added up. If we dialed in, we would find that there are ten or fewer random failures behind the blanket statement that you "lack focus."

The Writing Habit

Right now, your goal is to write 20,000 words a day consistently. There are a couple of core skills that you need to develop to achieve this goal.

You need to be able to write quickly for short periods of time. You then need the ability to turn these sprints into longer writing blocks. During this transition, you move from tracking words per minute to words per hour.

Then you need the ability to maintain that pace for a marathon. Pretty much anybody can write quickly for five minutes. The real skill is turning those five-minute sprints into a two-hour writing session, then expanding until you are sprinting for three to four hours a day. That's when you start hitting some serious numbers.

Many possible distractions can get in the way. But let's focus on the most likely culprits. Most of our habit problems have to do with time allocation, focus, and priority.

When we misdiagnose one of these problems, we blame the universe or talents. We mix up talents and skills all the time. You can improve and learn new skills, but talents are things we are born with.

Skills = random

Talent = systemic

There is a simple test to measure if the problem is a lack of ability.

When you're telling yourself that you don't have the ability to write 20,000 words in a day, apply this test. If a loved one's life were on the line, could you crank out those words? Of course you could.

This test proves that the problem is fixable. You can improve with more time or focus.

The Power of Ritual

Once you have isolated your cause of failure, you can begin to fix it. Your failure is the result of distraction and that's simply a bad habit.

To deal with a habit-based problem, I like to start with ritual. "Ritual" is a very powerful word, and it's much better to use than habit. It's such an unfamiliar word that I can use its power to help you become a faster writer.

Rituals are very specific and well defined. A ritual must be performed in a certain order using a certain length of time. This specificity provides power.

We are going to develop a ritual together right now. This will be the ritual you perform before every single writing session. Using a ritual in this way will help you get into the zone faster every single time you write.

It is very hard for me to tell you to start the habit of writing 20,000 words a day now. That's a big goal, and it requires a big habit. Even telling you to write two-hour blocks at a time might overwhelm you. Large goals require large habits, and those are overwhelming.

The secret to large habits is the same as the secret to writing a large book; break it down into smaller pieces. Small habits stack into large habits. And the best way to build those small critical habits is to wrap them in a ritual.

If you start every writing session with a cup of tea at the same time, if you regulate what time you eat during the day, if you control what time you start and finish each task, you begin to create a ritual. You can call it habit stacking if you prefer that term, but in my opinion, a collection of habits is a ritual.

Put together a series of actions that you repeat around every writing session. These small tasks will build the emotional infrastructure that you need to build your new habit. You don't build a new skyscraper without scaffolding. We need a support structure in place.

Before we think about having a ritual, we must prepare our tools. Complete your outline, have it in a usable format and complete all of your research. These steps need to be completed, or your writing session is destined to fail.

Design Your Ritual

Begin to create a ritual that you perform before each writing session. The exact nature of the ritual doesn't matter. It's the act of performing a series of steps in a very particular pattern.

When your ritual is specific and strict, it becomes powerful. My ritual even involved listening to the same songs repetitively. Now, I write in such large sessions that my ritual covers the entire day. But for now, start with a small pre-writing ritual.

If you already created your ritual back during the section on getting into the zone, wonderful! If not, now you have a second chance to use this technique to build powerful habits.

Action Steps

1. Memorize the two types of failure.

2. Analyze the barriers that have kept you from hitting your writing targets in the past.

3. Have you blamed your failures on third parties? Has this limited your ability to change your destiny?

4. Apply the "The Sudoku Mom Gun Test" to each of your past excuses and see if it really is beyond your ability to turn things around.

5. Look for the causes of failures in your own habits and isolate each one.

6. Build a writing ritual and be very strict about it.

BREAKING BAD

Desire is the key to motivation, but it's determination and commitment to an unrelenting pursuit of your goal - a commitment to excellence - that will enable you to attain the success you seek.
- Mario Andretti

Stop and Go Systems

Within your brain, your habits are controlled by two primary systems; one system forms habits and the other stops them. Your brain is designed to create maximum efficiency, so your habit-formation system is far stronger than your habit-stopping system.

This weak system explains why so many people are trapped in bad habits.

Instead of stopping bad habits, we simply replace them with good ones.

Brain Macros

Your brain uses habits to store shortcuts just like your computer does. On the computer, these shortcuts are called macros. You push one button, and the computer takes several actions.

This habit-formation system is designed to decrease how much of the day you spend thinking about things that don't matter. Breathing is a habit. Your heartbeat is also a habit. We don't have the ability to control our heartbeats, but you do have some ability to control your breathing. As we move higher up the function tree, we have more control over our habits.

Stopping Addiction

Starting and forming habits is a lot easier than quitting them. Learning to smoke only takes a few minutes, but quitting takes some people decades.

Your habit-stopping system is very weak and is powered by your ability to focus. If the only thing you're thinking about is quitting smoking twenty-four hours a day, seven days a week, the habit-stopping system will work. But if you become stressed, if you become distracted by anything else, then the system will fail. Its great weakness is that your habit-stopping system only works when you actively think about it.

The solution to this age-old conundrum is habit replacement. We want to take bad habits and replace them with good ones.

Infrastructure

This process begins with building up the correct infrastructure. Depending on your situation, you will be dealing with different distractions and bad habits.

For every habit, there is a distraction that keeps us from achieving success. Perhaps you can't hit your daily workout goal. Maybe you are always late for work. Maybe you just watch way too much television.

Whatever your habit problem, it can be fixed by focusing on infrastructure first.

When I was a senior in high school, I stopped watching television altogether. I had a revelation that television is a mind suck because there is no beginning and no end. You can sit in front of the television all day, every day and be entertained and distracted forever.

This was long before there were DVRs. So I switched from watching television to watching DVDs. I signed up for Netflix and would only watch them on my television. Some people look at this and can't see the difference. But I created several infrastructure gates to limit my wasted time. First, movies have a beginning and an end. When the movie is over, you have to walk up to the machine, take the old movie out, put a new video in and press play. You must actively decide to watch more. Additionally, starting a new movie is a commitment to stay still for at least ninety minutes. Instead of losing eight hours a day, in short, thirty-minute blocks, I had to actively decide if I wanted to spend another two hours watching a movie.

The more infrastructure we can place between you and the bad habit, the better. If you are watching TV when you should be working, then we can slowly replace that habit with better habits. The first is to move away from watching live television. There is nothing worse than watching television live. You are spending 20 to 30 percent of your time watching commercials. That's not entertaining!

The first step is to switch from watching live to watching recorded versions of your shows. Just waiting to watch a show until right after it has ended will recapture precious minutes of your life.

The path to success is replacement. Replace your live habit with recorded versions. That's the first replacement, and you get back about 25 percent of that wasted time. This is a much easier first step to implement. The second advantage to watching recorded shows is that you have to actively decide to watch each show by clicking that button on your remote. We are turning your passive bad habit into an active one. We are building some great infrastructure.

Focus Tools

When it comes to focusing on your computer, there are many tools out there designed to help you. New software is constantly being designed to help you focus and avoid distraction.

There are different tools that can block the Internet, turn off certain programs or turn off everything on your computer except for a word processor. Some programs are time-based, and some are goal-based, so you can't close the program until you hit your word count goal.

These types of software tools range from mild to very aggressive, and by testing different tools you may find one that helps you maintain your focus. I don't use one, but they are out there.

Rather than using tools, I prefer to tackle my distractions one by one. The problem with these tools is that they don't remove the desire. The reason I quit smoking so effectively was not because I removed access to cigarettes. People who try that always fail. Instead, I removed the desire.

Unconscious Habits

Let's begin by removing and replacing our distractions one at a time. One of my biggest distractions for a very long time was email, and it destroyed my productivity. I felt it was crucial to be reachable at all times.

In reality, I was wasting a lot of time responding instantly to unimportant emails and checking my phone when there were no new messages.

Many of us have an unconscious habit with our cell phones. We check them all the time throughout the day. If I told you to turn off your cell phone for the next twenty-four hours, most likely you would still have moments where you feel the need to check it.

Checking our phones has become an uncontrollable habit.

The Power of Motivation

Motivation requires three elements: energy, strategy, and a clearly defined goal.

How badly do you want to make this change? How much energy and excitement do you feel about changing your bad habits for good? The more energy you start with, the easier it is to stay the course. But energy alone isn't enough.

This is where strategy comes in. We need to develop and implement an effective strategy if we want to achieve success. Quitting habits is a bad strategy, but replacing them is a good strategy. You have now mastered this component.

The final problem comes from how we set goals. Most people have an ill-defined desired result. There is a big difference between "I want to write faster" and "I want to write 20,000 words a day." Most of us set vague goals that merely point in a direction, with no way to measure success. The second problem with most goal-setting is that we set goals that are too far into the future.

Achieving success with one big goal is impossible. It's not achievable. Instead, you must break down each day into a series of small goals. You can form habits by targeting small goals.

We activate habits through repetition. When you do the same thing repetitively, your brain stores that behavior as a macro and it becomes automatic.

Our lives are filled with little habits that we never think about. Nearly everyone on earth sleeps with their feet toward the door. Have you ever thought about why you do this?

There are things in our lives we don't think about that we could change if we put our minds to it. The only way to achieve your goals is to break them down into smaller, achievable goals. Our brains are far better at focusing on short-term goals than long-term. Short-term desire overwhelms long-term need.

Let's circle back to the core reason you are reading this book. You want to be able to write quickly. When you can write fast, you shorten the distance between setting the goal of writing a book and hitting that goal. The shorter that cycle, the more powerful your ability to focus on that goal.

When it takes six months or more to write a book, each goal is very far away. It's hard to divide up the time between now and that far-away goal effectively. But when writing a book only takes two weeks, you can organize your time very efficiently. The closeness of the goal feels much more real.

Life Gets in the Way

Sometimes life will get in the way, and if your goal for writing is far away, that can be devastating.

When you have complete control over how fast you write, you can begin to manage your days in the same way. When you know how many words you can write in a day, controlling the output becomes very manageable. You can see exactly how far away the goal is every day.

However, if that goal is far off, it's hard to be precise. If this book were six months from completion, then I would lose focus all the time. I would take days off and think that they don't matter, but then the book would end up taking nine months. If we are too far away from our goals, it becomes very easy to lose the course.

We must create clearly defined and measurable short-term goals. Each of these smaller goals is a component of that larger long-term goal of writing 20,000 words a day. Now, do you understand why I taught you to write in short sprints multiple times per day? I'm breaking up each day into smaller, manageable goals for you.

Action Steps

1. Concentrate on forming new habits rather than quitting bad ones.

2. Isolate the habits that are impeding your progress and replace them.

3. Start with small steps; don't try to make massive change in a single day.

4. Experiment with focus software to see if that helps you improve your skills.

5. Focus on replacing the desire for bad habits rather than the access.

6. Divide big goals into small, daily tasks. The more small tasks, the better.

7. Be prepared for some slip-ups along the way, but don't use that as an excuse to quit.

SETTING GOALS

If you set your goals ridiculously high and it's a failure, you will fail above everyone else's success.
   - James Cameron

The Right Way

Most of our failures can be traced back to how we set goals. When we fail to set goals correctly, failure becomes inevitable. We tend to set vague, far-away goals and then we're shocked when we fail. The problem is that these goals are just too vague. They don't feel very real.

   Your goal right now might be to write a book. That's an admirable goal, and it feels solid because the result is clear. Either you write the book, or you don't. You can clearly measure if you have succeeded. The problem is that goal is too broad. How many pages will the book be? How many chapters? When do you want the book finished?

   When we don't set concrete goals, they change over time. Your memory is unreliable. Your desire to make yourself feel good will prevent you from achieving what you want and deserve.

It's time to start creating achievable goals.

Instead of telling yourself, "I want to write a book," say, "I want to write a book that's 90,000 words long, and I want to finish it in the next thirty days." What you've created is an effective goal.

We want a goal that includes real numbers because then we can divide it into pieces. When you say you want to have a book that's 90,000 words done in thirty days, you know you need to write 3,000 words a day to hit your goal.

Break Goals into Days

Be very specific when setting your goals. This allows you to take each target and slice it into daily tasks. Writing 90,000 words in a month sounds very daunting, but writing three thousand tomorrow isn't nearly as intimidating. We can take a goal that seems impossible and make it manageable by breaking it down into daily tasks.

Now is a magnificent time to set your next writing goal in stone. How many words is your next project? How fast do you want to complete it?

The smaller our goals are, the more frequently you will get the positive reinforcement of having achieved a goal. Now that we have a daily goal, we want to go even smaller.

Tiny Goals and Multiple Projects

The secret to my success as a writer is my ability to make tiny goals. Getting down to daily goals is really good, and most people only go that far, but I need more. I want to break my goal down into dozens of goals I can accomplish every day. My favorite way to do this is with the program Scrivener. Switching from Word to Scrivener tripled my writing speed and job satisfaction.

I love writing with Scrivener because it allows me to create hundreds of miniature goals within each project. I can hit dozens of writing goals every day.

It's very possible to achieve your goals when you structure them properly. Take your daily goal and break it down into smaller pieces. Set a goal for each writing sprint. If you need to write 3,000 words today, break that into three sprints of 1,000 words each. If that's too much, break it down into four sprints. As long as you sit down at the computer with a target in front of you, it's achievable. It is far better to finish five out of your six sprints and end the day with 2,500 words than to try a massive single sprint that wears you out. It is critical that you avoid burnout.

Once you have broken your day down into smaller pieces, go one step further. Break your project into as many pieces as possible. Before it was a bestseller on Amazon, *Serve No Master* was a Scrivener file with over 190 sections. My average section is 500 words. Each time I write 500 words I click on an icon to move to the next section.

This is a critical moment. Each time I finish a section I get a little hit of euphoria. That feeling of accomplishing a goal makes me feel good.

Instead of writing to a timer or word count, I work my way through a folder, and when I'm done, I can close that folder. I know that I don't have to look there again, and that feels magnificent.

This gives me a feeling of accomplishment, but it also helps me stretch myself. When I'm feeling a little tired and thinking of quitting, I push myself to at least finish that folder. When it's done, I can turn off the computer for the day and feel really good about myself.

You can break your goals down by word count, time, or sections. I like to do all three. This means that I get that good feeling several times an hour. It's a great way to stay motivated.

Ritual

I've already mentioned that I'm a big believer in ritual. It's the key to maintaining your writing habit. Writing is a lonely profession, and without structure, distraction can quickly rear its ugly head. This is the first time I've ever written a book outside, using dictation. But I already have a ritual.

I start by putting on my recording clothes. I make sure that I have the equipment that I need to take with me prepared ahead of time. I always take my slippers off at the exact same spot on the dock. I set everything down in the same place, and I always do things in the same order. Not because I have some type of O.C.D. problem; it's the opposite.

My mind suffers from entropy. I have to impress structure on the chaos around me in order to maintain my habits. There's a huge part of me that would love to turn off this recording, set everything down, and jump in the water; to swim right now and just enjoy the ocean. Only my infrastructure of habit and ritual is keeping me here with you.

Instead of just focusing on one massive habit, start small. You can build your rituals one step at a time. When you have one small habit, you can easily measure success. The key to every part of this process is making your goals, habits, and targets as small as possible.

Here is a simple but powerful writing ritual example.

Every day, I put on my special writing hat. Then I drink a cup of tea and listen to my favorite song. I then go to the bathroom and from there, straight to my writing nook.

This might seem simple, but this ritual is enough to prepare your body to write. You will find getting into the zone very easy.

You can also establish infrastructure to keep your focus. Checking email once a day is part of my infrastructure. My early morning email ritual has replaced my old, bad habit of checking my email constantly. With this tactic, you get the task done and then the distraction is removed for the day.

Infrastructure

As you experiment with the best times of day for writing, the best methods and locations, you will find what works best for you. When you have found the best writing situation for you, plan out your goals, micro goals, and rituals. Build your infrastructure and set it in stone.

All these steps work together to make your goals achievable. Your ritual can become part of your daily goal structure. It should be an integrated part of your life.

Breaking your ritual into pieces helps you relax. Thinking about how much you have to write today or your next sprint can be overwhelming. If you get nervous, your writing will suffer.

The power of ritual is that it requires focus. We establish rules for each phase of the ritual, and they become sacrosanct. When you drink that tea, only think about that tea. You aren't allowed to think about work. It's against the rules.

"This is my cup of tea, and this tea is very important to me. I never write while I drink my tea. This time is precious."

It's not the tea itself that becomes important, but how you approach each step in your ritual. During your pre-writing ritual, it's forbidden to think about work. Don't think about the future or that next scene. This will keep your ritual pure and ensure that when you sit down at your computer or turn on your microphone, you are relaxed and ready to slip into the zone.

If you have followed the rest of this process and turned your giant project into small, 500-word sections, then you can stay relaxed. You transition from your ritual to a small writing goal. You don't have to think about a giant book, deadlines, or your goal of writing 20K today. You can just focus on that one section, and this will keep you relaxed.

Just think about one goal at a time. Combining ritual with proper goal-setting leads to perfect habit development. My friend Steve calls this process habit stacking, but I've always called it ritual.

We build a series of things we do that end with our habit of success.

Action Steps

1. Set your first writing goal now and be very specific. Include a word count and a due date.

2. Break down all your current goals into smaller, manageable pieces.

3. Continue building and refining your ritual until it is perfect.

4. Use your small goals and new ritual to transition into the zone each time you start a writing session.

5. Keep track of your writing results when you use your ritual and when you don't. Always track your results in your notebook.

6. Create an infrastructure that the people you live with understand, so that you are able to keep your ability to get into the zone protected.

ENERGY

I believe in luck and fate and I believe in karma, that the energy you put out in the world comes back to meet you.
 - Chris Pine

Creative Flow

As a writer, you need a steady flow of creative ideas coming into your mind. You need to actively bring the right kind of creativity into your flow. I read an entire book nearly every day. Running thousands of words through my mind keeps my ideas fresh.

I'm always absorbing new ideas, knowledge, and information. Reading is the best way to maintain and grow my vocabulary.

Reading is a habit that helps me with my career, and it is also a great pleasure. I love reading because it gives me knowledge while recharging my emotional batteries.

I also get a great deal of my emotional energy and inspiration from living on a paradise tropical island and being able to work outside, spend time with my family, and being able to work from home. All of these things bring me positive energy.

Poisoning the Well

As much as we want to bring positive, creative energy into our lives, we must be diligent about blocking negative energy from infecting us. The more we expose ourselves to negative energy, the more it can infect the way we think.

We all let things into our lives that affect us emotionally. For some people, it's politics. For other people, it's the feeling of always needing to know the news and what is going on in the world. It's hard to be in a good state of mind if you read a lot of intense political and news websites.

Affecting Your Emotions

The things we watch and the books we read affect our state of mind. They affect what we're doing. We must always pay attention to what we bring into our minds because it will affect our tone. If you notice that your tone is very negative, think about what you've let in.

It is important to set up habits that help us to stay in the right emotional state and to help us stay happy, healthy, and focused. Maintaining habits and hobbies is critical.

The Yin and the Yang

While you are writing, always pay attention to your emotional and psychological wellbeing. You will find the perfect balance that allows you to make a great living while enjoying your life.

You don't want to write so few words that you can't make a living from your writing, and you don't want to write so many words that you can't maintain it. That's the balance we seek.

A writing habit is about more than just the time in front of the computer. When building out the structure of your day, include time to take care of your mind, body, and spirit. To be a great marathon writer, you must develop a lifestyle that allows it. The time I spend not writing is even more critical than the time I spend hammering away at a keyboard.

Action Steps

1. Find a hobby that brings creative energy and ideas into your life.

2. Find a physical activity that recharges your batteries and keeps you healthy.

3. Push yourself to the limit to find how many words you can write when you have to "redline."

4. Pay attention to how books, movies and music affect your mood and your writing. Only listen to music that affects your writing when you need it.

5. Focus on going beyond the time you spend writing and create a lifestyle that you can maintain.

THE POWER OF POSITIVE REINFORCEMENT

Well, you know, a lot of people look at the negative things, the things that they did wrong and - which I do. But I like to stress on the things I did right, because there are certain things that I like to look at from a positive stand-point that are just positive reinforcement.

- Tiger Woods

Christmas Eve

No matter the size of the goal, the anticipation of hitting it sometimes feels even better than actually hitting it.

We enjoy the anticipation more than the moment after because once we've achieved the goal, there's nothing left to look forward to. This is something I struggled with this as an early writer. My first goal was to sell one book; now my goals are much bigger.

Writing Addiction

There are certain things that I've mentioned throughout this book that we're going to start bringing together in the final phases.

When you're writing, if you only have one big goal at the end of your project, you don't get to feel good until you've reached the end. We have the same chemical reaction whether we accomplish a big or small goal, which is why we should set several smaller goals for ourselves.

Breaking down your writing projects into small goals gives you constant rewards. You can work in a state of perpetual satisfaction as you hit many goals.

Bar Example

We can either be glass half-full or glass half-empty people. The more we become glass half full people, the easier life will become. I don't want you to focus on the long-term goal you haven't accomplished yet.

By looking at the goals we haven't achieved, we are focused on the unfinished goal, which forces us into a negative emotional state.

Not hitting goals does not mean failure; it means we're learning. Whenever you have a random failure or an incomplete goal, that's not a sign of failure; that is a sign of progress. You're climbing up the mountain.

It doesn't matter if you fail according to someone else, as soon as you feel bad about goals you didn't hit, you make your job exponentially more challenging.

You must attach positive emotions to the act of trying.

The Act of Trying

Do whatever it takes to maintain your emotional health.

By chopping up a large goal into small goals and rewarding yourself along the way, you will be rewarding yourself with a continual feeling of success. This process is a tactic that trains you to attach positive emotions to effort.

If you sit down at your computer tomorrow and only write one sentence, that is not a failure. You did not fail because at least you tried.

Trying is the first step on the path to success.

When you have the ability to attach positive emotions to your efforts, it will change your life. You will become capable of much more.

Action Steps

1. Are you constantly chasing that next emotional high?

2. When you try and fail, do you focus on the failure or the trying?

3. How many projects have you quit because of these negative emotions?

4. Break your big goals into small goals to give yourself a perpetual sense of accomplishment.

5. Attach positive feelings to the act of trying.

6. Be aware that social groups are another way negative emotions can slip in.

7. Develop a plan for fighting these negative emotions. Focus on the goals you accomplished today, look at your list of lifetime successes, and do whatever it takes to keep yourself positive.

DICTATE YOUR BOOK

If I have an idea, I write it down, although I usually carry a little dictation machine with me because I'm too lazy to write.
   - Tommy Shaw

Living in the Future

There are a few key reasons why you should consider adding dictation to your repertoire. The first and the most important reason is because the technology has finally arrived. Now the technology exists to dictate without the need for a secretary or a transcriptionist.

In the past, dictation technology did not work as well as it does today. It has improved tremendously over the years.

Health

Learning the skill of dictation can also protect you from medical ailments such as wrist, elbow, knee, and back pain from sitting too long. Dictating gives you the freedom to get away from sitting in a chair in front of a computer for long periods of time.

You don't have to sit at your desk to work because you can dictate from any location. You are no longer chained to your laptop.

Unique Challenges

Dictation is not the ultimate panacea that will solve every problem for new writers. Many places writers prefer to work will become off limits because of noise or crowds of people. You can't dictate in a coffee shop, on the subway, or in a crowded bar because you have to remain conscious of other workers and background noise.

Distraction-Free Writing

We all have our favorite distractions. Working from home leaves a person vulnerable to temptation. Whether you are sitting at your desk, in front of the computer, or on the couch, temptation is only seconds away.

Thirty years ago, entertainment options on a computer were limited. Computers were mainly used for work. In the decades since, everything has changed. Computers have become many people's primary entertainment source.

When you are trying to work with the same tool you use for entertainment, of course you are going to struggle to focus. There are too many distractions - from hopping around the internet to looking at pictures, to reading email or just playing games. Social media alone can make your entire day disappear. There are a million different ways your computer can distract you.

When you're dictating, you move away from all of the digital distractions. Working away from temptation is so much easier.

When I am dictating, there are no spell checks or grammar checks to underline words in red. Both layers of temptation disappear. The temptation to edit is also eliminated because it's impossible to edit on the fly.

The more you separate the creative and the technical processes, the easier it will be for you to achieve success. Dictation allows you to do that.

The Oral Tradition

Have you ever been working on a chapter in your book, and you just can't seem to get it right, but if you tell your friend what you want to happen, it suddenly becomes easy?

There's something about telling a story out loud that's a little bit more natural for us. You might find that it's easier for you to tell stories and that they flow better when you speak them out loud.

Action Steps

1. Take a look at different dictation software and apps on the 20K page.

2. Experiment with some free tools.

3. Find your perfect recording location.

4. Look at using software versus paying people to transcribe for you.

5. Do you have a family member you can get to transcribe for you?

6. Experiment with a tough chapter and see if speaking is easier than writing.

TRANSITIONING INTO DICTATION

There is nothing so stable as change.
 - Bob Dylan

Baby Steps

Trying to transition from writing to dictation all at once is a big mistake. Don't make massive changes to your workflow overnight. It's better to get comfortable with dictation before you decide to change to it forever.

If you are in the middle of writing a book, don't suddenly try and shift everything to dictation. Begin by shifting some of your side work first or start dictating your emails.

Part of the learning process is training the software to recognize your unique language. During the transition period, you will train the software to recognize your personal vocabulary. You will create a unique dictionary that matches your language style.

The software also must train you. With anything new there is a small learning curve. There are certain commands which generate punctuation. You need to know these or you will go insane hitting the period key all the time.

I am experimenting with transcribing into the computer, but so far I'm still just dabbling. I always want to share my personal experiences with you so you know that I am not giving advice that I don't follow myself.

Finding the right rhythm will take time and experimentation. Don't jump into something you aren't ready for because effective change is more important than fast change. If you try to change too much too quickly, it may be too hard, and you may end up quitting.

As long as you take it slowly and give yourself the ability to switch back to your keyboard anytime you feel frustrated, you can be successful with dictation.

Dictation is Optional

You don't have to dictate to write fast. The majority of the techniques and processes in this book will work without using your voice. You can still hit 20,000 words a day using your keyboard.

Any aspect of writing that diminishes your joy is a problem. Writing fast doesn't have to be hard, painful, or unpleasant. If you don't enjoy writing a book, how will someone else enjoy reading it?

As you master the skill of writing fast, focus on mastering one skill at a time. Don't overwhelm yourself.

Don't let yourself become frustrated. As soon as you've hit that moment where you lose your flow and dictating becomes difficult, switch back to hand writing your book. The journey is just as important as the destination.

You can always come back to dictation tomorrow when you are feeling refreshed.

Action Steps

1. Transition to dictation slowly.

2. Start experimenting with dictation sprints.

3. Make a plan for switching back to typing when you start to feel frustration mounting.

4. Find a workflow that works for your rhythm and master it.

5. Alternate between typing and dictation sprints.

JUMPING INTO DICTATION

Living at risk is jumping off the cliff and building your wings on the way down.

- Ray Bradbury

Start Small

Our initial goal with dictation is to increase how quickly you can generate the same number of words as you do when typing by hand.

Most of the processes in the 20K system are for writing by hand. You research, create outlines, take notes, and build mind maps by hand.

Dictation is simply about helping you to generate words faster. Instead of working five or six hours a day you can just work one or two and produce the same number of words.

Choose the best workflow for you. You don't need to replicate your favorite author to become a master of your craft. Everyone has a unique way of thinking, learning, and creating. We want to maximize your natural potential.

Test Your Workflow Phases

Once you've decided the workflow that you want to experiment with, you will move into further phases of experimentation. Your current workflow is merely a baseline, and you should always be looking for ways to improve each part of your process. Once you have a baseline, break down your writing process into distinct phases and experiment with replacing each one with dictation.

Decide where you're going to use dictation in your process, but don't use it everywhere. Eventually, you may move into a world of total freedom from your keyboard, but it will take more than one day.

The biggest limitation on dictation is going to be your body. If you start speaking eight hours straight every day, you will get a sore throat and hurt your voice. Start simple and slowly to bring dictation into your process.

Add a Cleanup Phase

With dictation and transcription, you're going to need a cleanup phase. This phase is no joke; that is the biggest lesson from my great dictation experiment. It took me several tries to get a workable draft, and editing this book has taken much longer than any project I've ever worked on in the past.

Whether you clean up your text yourself, have an assistant do it, or find someone to handle the entire transcription process for you, you must add that phase into your workflow. It's a new phase that we don't have when typing.

Editing is a primary phase, but with dictation, you need to slip a new step in front of your editing process. This is where you fix any transcription errors and add in missing punctuation.

At first, I thought that the cleanup phase for this book would be easy. I wrongly assumed that it was a labor-intensive task that any English speaker could handle.

Cleaning up the transcription from Dragon required a great deal of decision-making. Even though the draft had a small percentage of mistakes, they started to add up. Several times, I had to go back and listen to my audio recording.

The cleanup phase is a new hurdle, but I love sitting outside and dictating so much that I will find a way to make it work.

Get the Equipment

With whichever workflow you choose, the quality of your microphone will affect the quality of your final product. If you use a low-quality microphone, there will be more mistakes in the transcriptions. One of the problems that I had during my initial foray into Dragon was the result of using a low-quality headset. Unfortunately, I didn't realize it for a while and I blamed my problems on technical glitches.

A decent microphone is an investment in your business and worth the cost. I'm a big believer in spending from profit, not from debt. You can record your first book using a simple setup and then invest in better equipment from the profits of that book. That can be your reward for doing awesome with your first dictated book!

Find Your Voice

As you try different things, you will discover what works for you. You might be amazing at dictating outlines and terrible at dictating dialogue scenes. That's OK. We want to know that information.

Use dictation as a supplement to speed up different parts of your workflow. If it slows you down or decreases your speed in different areas, then don't use it in that area. I don't use dictation when editing because it would slow me down massively.

Knowing your limitations is very important, and you only find them through experimentation. I want to show you as many options as possible for designing your workflow so that we discover the one that's perfect for you.

Dragon Tips

I record training videos nearly every day. When recording a video using my computer, I have no problem using my natural voice. I am speaking to people, and the computer is just the recorder. When I start dictating to the computer, however, my voice starts to get a little robotic. I have to fight against this urge to maintain the quality of my work.

When dictating directly to the computer, get comfortable with the voice commands. Certain phrases cause the computer to do something other than writing them on the page. Other than these, you can create a custom dictionary for special words and specific commands that you use frequently. The more time you invest in the software, the better it will perform.

You can insert dictation into any part of your workflow, and that decision will affect how you work with your software. It boils down to creating a different profile for each different microphone, taking the time to train the software, and using your natural speaking voice.

Action Steps

1. Learn to use your dictation software. Start with a list of the main "command" words.

2. Start with just one hour a day.

3. Train with your computer to improve the performance of your software.

4. Focus on speaking without using your robot voice.

5. Create a user profile for each microphone, person, and recording location.

6. Check your hardware before you blame your software. Sometimes a slow computer or bad microphone is the culprit. (Make sure the right microphone is activated.)

7. Be very conscious of your body and stop if your throat gets sore or dry.

GO MOBILE

A smartphone is a mobile computer in your pocket.
  - Nick Woodman

Smartphone Dictation

Let's talk about untethering. In this section, we are going to dig into recording your audio away from a computer. When on the road or not in your office, you can record using many different apps. All you need is a smartphone and the world is your office.

Sound Good - Posture

There are a few ways to ensure that your mobile recordings go as smoothly as possible.

Start with the way you sound. I have learned that we speak differently based on our body position. If you're lying down, you speak very slowly and calmly. As you move your body upright, you become more active and energetic.

Try different body positions to see what works best for you. Many authors find that standing while recording gives them more energy.

Once you find the position that works right for you, you want to test for consistency. For 90 percent of this book, I'm sitting in the same position because your body position affects the tone of your voice.

Standing, sitting, lying down or walking around, choose the body position that's right for you.

System Crash

I've experienced so many technical disasters that I live in a constant state of paranoia. I've lost recordings and files too many times to let it happen to you. There's nothing worse than recording the perfect ending to your book and then watching your computer crash before it saves your file.

I've lost recordings of a ninety-minute webinar in the past, and it's devastating. Now I record each live session with three or four backup methods. I've had two different backups fail on the same night.

In my experience, dictation software autosaves every few minutes. You always have rolling backups, and even a system crash will only lose you a few minutes of work. With audio recording programs, however, there is no backup. Most recorders don't save until you hit stop at the end of a session. If something goes wrong in the middle of your epic recording session, there is no backup.

You can take action now to protect yourself from disaster. No matter how you record your audio, stick to small sessions.

Technical Trauma

Always check your setup before you start recording. Every time you record, check your settings. It is a horrible feeling to record for an hour to realize your audio is ruined or you used the wrong microphone.

Before you get into the content, record yourself for fifteen seconds and play it back to make sure everything sounds great. Check your settings at the start of each recording session. Don't assume that just because they were right yesterday, they've stayed the same. I can't stress this enough: double-check everything.

Backups

Back up your outlines, your recordings, and your equipment. If you only have one microphone and something goes wrong, you can't work for the day. If your microphone uses batteries, always have backups with you. Backing up equipment is critical here because ordering a replacement can take up to two weeks. That's a long time to be out of business.

If you can afford it, it's worth having extra microphone cables, extra batteries, a backup microphone, and different setups. I want to be able to record if the Internet crashes, my laptop dies, or the power goes out. I try to think ahead so that I don't lose time when disaster strikes.

Smartphones

Over the years, I've upgraded different parts of my home studio. Some things stay the same, and some things change. I've been using the same microphone and video camera setup for seven years for my outdoor videos.

Recently I have started dabbling with recording videos using my iPhone. The quality is way better than I expected.

Other than this experiment I have been using the same video camera since I started in this business back in 2010. I'm still waiting for a better camera to enter the market.

Video Cameras

There's nothing comparable to this camera, and everything that's come out since is either more expensive or more complicated. Most newer models don't have an input for an external microphone, and that's unacceptable to me. When I knew that the video camera was going to be discontinued, I bought three of them. I already have two lavalier microphones that connect to that model and sound fantastic.

Even if something goes wrong with one of my microphones I have a backup. I like to back up microphones and power supplies as much as possible.

The Right Gear

When you're going mobile and leaving the house to record, keep your notes on a separate device. Don't use your phone to store your outline and record. For podcast episodes, I write all my notes by hand in a spiral-bound notebook.

For this project, I stored all of my notes in my iPad mini. I very rarely use this device, even though I bought it five years ago. I don't get to use it very often because I don't go mobile that often. This purchase I made many years ago is finally paying off.

The notes for this book are far more extensive than the sketches for podcast episodes. It would take me longer to write these notes by hand than it's taking to record the entire book.

Don't run any other apps while you are recording. If you are recording and accidentally click an app that has sound or uses the microphone, it will disconnect your recording app. When I'm listening to music and open the wrong app on my phone, it disconnects the music.

Finally, there is the risk of disaster. Everyone has dropped their phone at least once. If I drop my phone into the ocean, I don't want to lose my recording and all my notes. That would be devastating.

Be Fastidious

The more you are fastidious from the start, the easier the dictation process will be. At the start of each recording, say the date, chapter name, section name and the title of your book. This will help if your file names get corrupted. Some programs save each file with the same name. And sometimes you forget to name the file you're recording. Including this reference data in the actual recording will protect you in case anything happens to your file structure. It's another layer of backup.

I give memorable names to every section in my books, fiction and nonfiction, to ensure that I know what's happening. I might change the section titles later on, but during the draft phase, it helps to use clear and descriptive names. It can be something as simple as "Prince Philip Gets Angry" or "Philip Fights Susan." Just saying that at the start of the recording will remind me of what happens in the scene. I don't have to listen to the whole recording to remember.

Having descriptive starts to each audio file allows me to sync them up with my Scrivener files. Sometimes the recording numbers get out of order. I always move around chapters and sections within chapters. The order of this book is not the order in which I recorded the sections.

You can never be too prepared with naming and organizing your files. With your first book, you can get away with being fast and loose with your organization. But once you've written ten, you'll have to go back and try to untangle your Gordian Knot.

Be Organized

Organize your hardware the same way you organize your files and software. Once you have a mobile audio setup that works for you, store your gear together.

Since all my equipment is in one place, and I can always find it. If something is missing, the shape of the hole is a big clue.

At the very least, designate a bag as your recording bag. If you always use the same bag, you'll be quicker to notice if anything is missing. When you load your recording bag, you can check for each thing you need to have.

Having all of your gear organized will prevent a technical problem or missing cable from shutting down your work. I wasn't properly prepared when I started recording this book. I started recording almost on the spur of the moment, and nothing was ready. My mobile setup is for recording video, so the wrong gear was organizing.

There were quite a few hiccups during that first day of recording. The iPad wasn't charged, I didn't have Scrivener on there for my notes, and there were a few other problems. Even with all my talk of preparation, I am still continuing to learn and improve my prep strategy.

I have a backup battery for my phone and iPad mini, but unfortunately my daughter thinks it is a toy phone, so it's always missing. I will have to buy another battery that doesn't look so fun as another layer of backup.

Prep Your Gear

I needed to charge the iPad, update the software, install the new version of the Scrivener app, and download the file from my computer to the iPad. It took quite a few hours to get everything done. It killed my afternoon because I didn't know I was going to start recording today. I wasn't prepared at all.

I have a very particular setup and know what I need when I record in the morning for my podcast episodes, and now I have a different setup to dictate these book chapters.

Whether it's a little case that protects everything, or a little travel bag, whatever you use, having a dedicated bag will make you more organized. Check the batteries on everything and have an extra battery pack on hand.

I know we have talked a lot about preparation and disaster. It's a big section because when it happens, it can be devastating.

Plan for disaster and distractions. Have a backup location and backup equipment. With enough preparation, external factors won't be able to hurt your ability to record.

Whenever you try a new recording location, check to see how the audio sounds. Check for wind and background noise. You might not even notice that cool breeze, but it could be enough to ruin your recording. Your software won't give you a usable transcription. You might need a better windscreen than the one that came with your microphone.

While I'm recording right now, people are playing soccer twenty feet behind one. A motorcycle just went roaring down the road. Everyone removes their mufflers here, so even a far-away motorcycle can find its way onto my recordings. And now a boat is cruising in front of me.

With all of that noise, I need to have my windscreen and audio settings correct. The quality is good enough to create a transcription.

Headphones

I know none of these noises are loud enough to mess with this recording because I've tested it numerous times, but I definitely couldn't use this recording for a podcast episode. I would never let anyone listen to this audio. If you want people to listen to the actual audio, it has to be pristine. Finding the right balance comes from experimentation and experience. Any time you go to a new location, record some samples and listen to them.

Don't listen through the device. If you listen to the speakers on your smartphone or the tiny, terrible speaker in your recorder, you won't be able to tell if the sound is good enough. Bad speakers will give you bad data.

Get the best headphones you can afford. I recently upgraded to some top of the line headphones. I bought the best Beats headphones I could find. They're Bluetooth, wireless, the battery lasts for ten hours, and they cover my ears enough to block unwanted noise. Whenever I listen to an audio file of my recording, I crank up the volume because I'm looking to hear what the bottom sounds like. The bottom is the lowest sound I want to hear.

If there's static, an electrical hum, or some background noise, you might not notice them if the audio is at low volume. However, when someone starts playing your audiobook in their car, they will hear those sounds. These same noises can confuse your dictating software and produce unreadable text. They can also torment your transcriptionist, if you hire a human.

If you're just listening to your computer speakers, you won't hear this noise when you test it. Cheap speakers don't transmit every frequency. Check audio on high-quality headphones to ensure you don't miss anything.

Turn the volume up to hear the sounds other than your voice. If there's too much background noise, it will affect everything. With dictation, we can get away with more background noise than when recording an audiobook.

Break a Sweat

When you're out and about, some people might look at you strangely when you're talking to yourself. This happens less and less these days; people are used to strangers taking public phone calls using hidden Bluetooth headsets.

Some people might think you're crazy for talking to yourself, but who cares? You're getting something important accomplished. You can get chores done or get exercise while writing your next book.

One caveat. Please don't jump straight into dangerous sports while dictating. If you want to break a sweat, go for a walk, but please don't go mountain climbing. I don't want to get an upset email from a family member after you fall. Avoid activities and sports that require concentration to stay alive.

I don't even walk very much while dictating; I'm pretty clumsy and will trip over a rock. I get so focused on what I'm saying that I lose track of my surroundings.

Find the right balance between enjoyment and focus. I would never be able to record this book while running or surfing, but you might be able to handle that easily. I can barely think when I'm exercising, let alone dictate a book.

I'm not ready to exercise and record at the same time. Maybe I'll be able to do it on a treadmill, but I certainly can't record while running on the beach.

If I'm running as fast as I can and panting, I can't speak in a normal voice and I won't get clean dictation. Sitting on my dock is the perfect balance for me, but if you're a natural athlete or marathon runner, you might find recording while you run quite easy. That's why we're testing – to find the perfect balance for you.

Dictation is One Piece

We've talked a lot about dictation in this book, but that's not the main thrust. Our main thrust is to find the techniques that turn you into the fastest writer possible. We covered all the writing techniques and drills first because they are more important. If you jumped right to this section, please circle back to the beginning. I covered some cool techniques you can use to get you faster.

Dictation cannot make up for errors in the rest of your writing strategies. It's an accelerator, not a replacement. Mix and match the different techniques from the 20K System to create your personal writing formula. Only then will you find writing nirvana.

Many people can double their words per hour quickly by using the 20K System, but that's not enough. Our goal is more than words per hour. We want to shrink the distance between starting and finishing your book. With the 20K System, you can finish the first draft of your novel in less than a month.

Speed is only one component of becoming a great writer. How quickly you can type or dictate is important, but it's not the whole story. Writing a book is about more than just throwing words onto a page.

If you only write for one hour a day, you're never going to hit your goals. We need to develop systems to turn you into a marathon writer. Focus on your daily word counts. That's where you will find massive success. Then you can start tearing through projects like a Tasmanian devil.

Design your day in a way that gets you the numbers you need. At this point, you may need to reread the sections on forming and developing habits. Writing successfully is a habit.

Part of my success comes from my writing speed, but another part comes from my tenacity. I stick with a task until it is finished and I always deliver projects on time.

I can focus on a project when I need to. When I get that middle-of-the-night phone call to write a book in four days, I know I can deliver.

I was not born with a great writing ability. I am very easily distracted. There are so many other things I'd love to do right now. Without strong habits and infrastructure, they would distract me, even from dictating on the beach. Without a strong habit, even dictation won't save your next writing project.

Having children changed my approach to business. With kids on the scene, I realized I have to start taking my career very seriously.

You go from making enough money to party this week to trying to make enough money to buy your kids food and diapers.

Strategies and techniques are powerful. They can accelerate your writing. But the writing habit is critical. Once you establish strong habits, your word counts will grow geometrically, and you will hit the goals you've always dreamed of.

Action Steps

1. Build your mobile recording studio. Organize your equipment and backups. Use the same bag or case every time you record.

2. Develop a pre-recording checklist. Check all your batteries and equipment.

3. Experiment with different postures and see how this affects your voice and tone. Use body position to improve your writing.

4. Modify your setup for multiple recording locations as different noises will impact your dictation accuracy.

5. Invest in backups and protection for your equipment.

6. Organize your files, equipment, and recordings.

7. Begin each recording with organizational data. Say the project name, date, chapter name and description for each section.

8. Test your equipment at the start of each recording session.

9. Get the best headphones you can afford to test your audio.

10. Experiment to find your perfect freedom, quality and exercise balance.

11. Go back through the habit section and build a dictation habit.

EDITING WITHOUT
TEARING YOUR HAIR OUT

*I write and write and write, and then I edit it down to the parts that I think
are amusing, or that help the storyline, or I'll write a notebook full of ideas
of anecdotes or story points, and then I'll try and arrange them in a way
that they would tell a semi-cohesive story.*
- Al Yankovic

Content is King

Who cares about editing? That was my first thought when I looked at
bringing in an external editor. Why should I pay someone to check
my spelling? I can just use spellcheck on Word and be done with it.

After seeing how many editors are absolutely ripping off up-and-
coming authors, I decided to stay as far away from them as possible.
Some editors will charge more than $10,000 to review your book.
Then they start talking about multiple passes, and an editor can
easily cost more than a new car.

I scored a near perfect score on the SAT in high school. On the

PSAT, I didn't make a single mistake in the English section. My master's degree is in teaching English. And yet I absolutely need an editor for one simple reason.

The Kiss of Death Review

I get a lot of bad reviews. Almost all of them attack me personally, and the most common complaint is that I'm a narcissist. I experiment on myself all the time, so I'm the main character in a lot of my examples. In some reviews, people will call me a jerk, say my book is boring and with the next breath say that I inspired them and changed their life.

I've only ever asked Amazon to remove one review. Someone figured out where I live and posted it. That's not ok; I'm extremely serious about my family's safety. I recorded an entire podcast episode about the time my family's safety was threatened by a website. You can find a link on the 20K page.

But let's not digress too far. These kind of bad reviews are annoying, but they won't kill a book. The kiss of death review is the sniper bullet directly into your cranium. It's a game-changer.

A review that points out grammatical and spelling mistakes is fatal. A single bad review that mentions anything technical will kill your sales. Be honest with yourself, when you see a book review that mentions bad spelling and grammar, do you still buy it? Me neither.

It's the ultimate way of calling an author a rank amateur. Amazon is the great equalizer and allows independent authors to compete with massive publishing houses. But one of these reviews will collapse the entire house of cards.

Most reviews are subjective. Some people are going to love your books, and some will hate them. It's impossible to have only five-star reviews. That world doesn't exist. But a review that attacks your grammar - that's objective. Everyone can agree that something is wrong with a book with these types of mistakes.

Avoiding the kiss of death review is worth every penny you pay your editor.

Types of Editing

When your first draft is complete, it's time to set aside the creative process. You have finished your rough draft, and that's great. Many authors get to this point and freeze. If you spend too much time writing that rough draft, it can be overwhelming to try and switch to editing mode. But you are not on this journey alone.

Together, we will go through a rather extensive process to take the book from rough draft to something we're releasing to the public. We will create a book that we are proud to publish and release into the world.

There are several distinct phases to the editing process. Going through each of these steps is where many new authors falter. Unfortunately, each of these stages is called editing and it can be a little confusing.

Even professional editors have different interpretations of the role of each type of editor. Sometimes, when you reach out to an editor and ask what they do, you'll find their definitions of an editor, line editor, copy editor, or proofreader is different.

If you hire an editor working from a different dictionary, they might do something totally unexpected.

The Cleanup Phase

If you dictated your book, we are going to need to add in one other stage: where you check the transcription and clean up the punctuation. The rougher your transcription, the rougher the cleanup phase will be. If you record your book remotely and then run it through Dragon Dictate, the cleanup phase could take longer than recording the actual book.

Dragon spits out giant blocks of text without any punctuation. Add in a few mistranslations and misinterpretations, and breaking that beast into usable text is a real fight. The text files for this book had no punctuation, no separation between sentences, and each recording was one giant paragraph of inscrutable text.

Based on my experience with cleaning up a 100,000-word book, I have changed this section quite a bit since recording on the dock. Attempts to pay someone else to clean up these files for me all failed. In the end, I had to clean up each section on my own. With a book this long, it became a miserable task. I began to dread working on a book that I loved writing so much on the beach.

If you transcribe directly into your computer, the cleanup stage is not a big deal. You added in punctuation along the way so that you can jump straight into traditional editing.

The easiest way to handle the cleanup phase is with a rolling process. Record remotely and each night when you come home, run a transcription through Dragon Dictate. Then run a cleanup on your work for the day. It won't take very long, and with everything fresh in your mind, you will easily decipher even the roughest of transcription errors.

If your book is under 20,000 words, then you can clean up your book rather easily at the end. Only for longer books do I recommend a rolling cleanup

Hiring a transcriptionist can be pretty expensive, so I know it's not an option for many authors. Hence, saving it for last.

I tried hiring people to clean up my transcriptions, but every effort failed. You should be prepared to put a lot of time into training your software to minimize mistakes. That effort upfront will save you a lot of pain down the road. Believe me, I wish I'd put a few days in working with Dragon rather than using the lazy approach. It really bit me in the bum.

Editors Galore

After the cleanup, it is time for the rewriting stages. This could very well be the first time you let an outsider see your book. You normally work with editors in this order:

1. line editor

2. copy editor
3. proofreader

If you are working with a publishing house, they may throw in a few other types of editors and even change this order, but if you are self-publishing, this is the most common order.

The Line Editor

A line editor is going to look at things like:

- Are you using too many words?
- Are your sentences too long and boring?
- Are you repeating yourself with different words?
- Is there any unnatural phrasing?
- Are there any confusing scenes or dialogs?
- Does the book go off-topic?

How many times have you read a book and the author explains the same thing three or four different times? It gets boring and feels redundant. Some authors do this across an entire series. They are so paranoid that a new reader will start with book seven in the series that they constantly re-explain each character's backstory and the rules of their universe. I don't need the author to explain how magic works in the universe seven or eight times per book.

Some authors go in the other direction. They write a series where you absolutely, positively must start with book one and read the stories in order. If you dare to start with book two, you will have no idea what's happening. Without knowing each character, you will be constantly confused.

I just started reading the second book in a science fiction series yesterday. I read book one a few months ago. Unfortunately, this book jumps right into an amazing battle scene and assumes that I know every character by name. There is no opportunity to refresh my memory. There's no chance for me to find out who these different characters are. It jumps right into the story.

It seems like I have to choose between remembering every character from books I read months or even years ago and getting each character's background dozens of times. Some authors constantly beat you over the head with the "rules" of their universe. If I remember who the characters are, I probably remember the science of this series.

If you are writing a series, the solution is to have a recap at the end of your book. Put a link at the beginning of the digital version that allows people to hop to the end and read it if they want. You can also include a dictionary that has a short biography of each character. Making this section optional is the best way to please new and old readers alike.

The line editor will help you walk that tightrope in your book between uninformative and boring. It's a tough balancing act. I live in dread that some readers will think I covered certain topics too many times in this book.

Your line editor is there to check for problems in dialogue structure, paragraph structure, and to point out scenes where the action is confusing.

Have you ever read a dialogue scene and after the first couple of back and forth discussions you can't tell who's talking?

I've read more than a few books where I can tell they didn't use a line editor because the dialog goes off the rails. It's annoying, but I understand why it happens.

A good line editor will catch all of these little mistakes and keep your audience from getting confused. They also look for strange changes in tone, weird phrasing, and bad or confusing language. Sometimes we are too descriptive and we use words that average people don't understand. Sometimes we're too bland, and we use words that don't have much meaning.

Occasionally we'll run into moments where our story goes down a rabbit hole. One of the things that happens to me (even in this book, I've probably done it a few times) is that I'll suddenly digress and talk about a different topic for too long, and it will feel like the central focus of this book has been lost. Hopefully my line editor will catch those moments and keep the book on track. The line editor is there to ensure that your pacing and language stay on track.

Copy Editor

After you finish with the line editor, it's time to dance with a copy editor. The copy editor corrects your spelling, grammar, punctuation, syntax, tense agreement, verb agreement, and every other grammatical error. They also check for consistency in spelling. A character's name should stay the same throughout your book, and "color" should not drift into "color."

You might have a word that you want to spell in a particular way. For example, I have a series of products on my website that I call Blueprints; Email Blueprint, Affiliate Blueprint, Blog Blueprint. In those cases, I always want to capitalize the B in Blueprint to let people know that it's part of the name of a product. If I sometimes have a lower-case b and sometimes have a capital B, that's weird. It's a mistake, and a good copy editor will chastise me.

A nonfiction copy editor checks for consistency and factually incorrect statements as well. If I make a claim in this book that's wrong because a new study has come out, the copy editor should catch that. They also check for internal consistency.

If at the beginning of this book I promised that you'd be able to write 10,000 words in a day, and at the end I promise 20,000, that's a little bit of internal inconsistency. That would need to be corrected.

The copy editor prepares the book for digital release. Once you have completed this phase, you can definitely upload your book to Amazon.

Proofreader

Most people mix up proofreader and editor, although they are quite different. The proofreader only steps in after the first copy of the book is printed.

If you use KDP Print to print the physical copies of your book, they will send you a proof of your book for anywhere between $2 and $7; the price depends on the length of your book and shipping.

The proofreader looks at the final copy of the book to see if there was a mistake in the printing process. When you move a book from digital to physical, the page numbers reverse. The page on the left on your computer becomes the page on the right in your book. All books in English start on the right side.

The biggest thing I check in the proofreading phase is page position. I don't want a table of contents on the left side with chapter one on the right. That looks weird.

With a digital book, a proofreader would read your book on their Kindle instead of inside a word processor. This allows them to replicate the reader experience.

Do I Really Need all these Editors?

Before you hire any editor, make sure that you agree on their job description. I rarely use three different people to edit one of my books. I almost never use a line editor because I write nonfiction; it's not as important for what I do. For certain projects, you need to bring in an external voice.

People email me all the time offering their editing services because they are masters of punctuation and grammar. They want to see the book before I release it into the world and are willing to help me out in exchange. I appreciate their offers to help, but I need line editing help more than I need copy editing help.

It helps me a lot when a reader can identify sections that are redundant or boring. I need help with the flow of a book this long far more than I need help with the grammar. I work with an amazing copy editor who catches most of my dumb mistakes.

Cost Control

Some editors are cripplingly expensive. There are editors who charge more to edit a book than I do to ghostwrite one! Before you hire anyone, ask them exactly what they do. Every editor is different.

They can charge anywhere from $1 per word to $1 per 10,000 words. Most editors have prices so high that independent authors could never afford them.

I know that you have a limited budget and don't want to give all of your profits to an editor, so in the following sections, I will share my editing process with you. This process is designed to minimize your costs and ensure that you avoid the kiss of death review. We are going to cover some cool ways to slash the cost of your editing process to the bone.

Watch the Clock

Have you ever wondered why some books announce their release days a year in advance? How does an author know in January that the book will be ready in November?

Allow me to let you in on a little secret. Editors can take a long time. Most editors take months to read a book. I see independent editors offering a turnaround of six to eight weeks. That means you have to wait two full months while someone else edits your book before you can release it.

I don't have the patience to wait two months to get my book back. I am in the business of selling books, so the moment a book is finished I want to start making money. I wrote *Serve No Master* in a week. I hate the thought of waiting eight times longer to get an edit back.

You can handle a large portion of the editing process yourself, getting you to your paydays way faster.

Action Steps

1. Clean up your dictation before you even consider reaching out to an editor.

2. Always confirm that your editor is going to do what you expect.

3. Never put yourself at risk for a "Kiss of Death" review.

4. Head over to the 20K page to see my tactics for finding great, affordable editors.

EDITING STAGE ONE - FIRST EDIT

Writing the last page of the first draft is the most enjoyable moment in writing. It's one of the most enjoyable moments in life, period.
- Nicholas Sparks

Handle it Yourself

You should handle the first editing stage yourself. If you dictated your book, clean up the first draft. I have links to transcription software and a few of the better services with reasonable prices on the 20K page. Some good transcription companies lower their rates over time. As you send more books, the price per minute goes down.

Once you have a completed rough draft, whether you typed or dictated the work, it's time to take a break. Spending some time away from your book will reset your brain.

I like to spend at least three days away from a book because that allows me to look at it with fresh eyes. If I start editing a book too quickly, I will have trouble mixing up memories of writing and editing. I might remember editing a chapter that is later in the book. This can cause discontinuity errors.

I might remember chapters out of order that will mess up my editing process. I can't give the book a fresh read if I don't take the time to cleanse my palate. I'm matching the customer experience. A little time away from your book between the creative writing phase and the analytical editing phase is critical.

Time is Ticking Away

Bringing in outside editors can add months to the book release cycle, and I don't have that kind of time; I try to release at least one book a month. Very few editors read as fast as I write; using three editors would push back my release dates by at least a full season.

When you go through a traditional publishing house, you will wait up to two years between book releases. An independent author trying to generate enough money to support a family doesn't have that kind of time. One of the keys to making a living as a writer is volume; the more books you self-publish, the more money you make.

Can you afford to wait two years between books? Of course not!

The whole purpose of the 20K System is to write 20,000 words a day. As discussed in the habit section, shrinking the time between starting a goal and achieving it is critical to success. If you can write a book in a month, adding three more months between that moment and publishing the book will destroy your focus. You will lose many of the benefits of the 20K System.

Feel

In order to control our time and costs, we want to handle as much of the editing process as possible ourselves.

There are some amazing tools designed to help fiction authors edit. Fiction authors can use scene maps, timelines, and character sheets to organize their books. I will post links to a lot of these tools on the 20K page.

With these additional tools, you can check how a scene is supposed to play out before you read it in your draft. These tools check that each scene has internal and external continuity and they allow you to track the pacing and ensure that the book follows your timeline.

With these different tools, you can check track your characters and ensure that the flow of the story makes sense.

There aren't as many specialized tools and techniques for nonfiction writing, so I have developed an approach from scratch. During this first rewrite, I focus on structure. I always reorganize my chapters a few times; the order that worked for the mind map doesn't always work for the final book.

Sometimes I find that a section exploded. In editing this book, some of my 500-word sections ballooned into 3,000 when I was dictating. During the first rewrite, I broke them into manageable pieces. Some of these sections even turned into chapters. You can't always predict where your book will go when you are writing that first outline.

Loops and Promises

A powerful writing technique is called loops or callbacks. These loops force people to read the entire book and keep them engaged all the way through the end.

The perfect example is the book that opens with an action scene and then rewinds to start the story a week earlier. To find out how that scene ends, the reader must work their way through the entire book.

My books are filled with loops that I open at the start of the book and close near the end. Each time I said, "I'll cover this a bit later," I was opening a loop with you. It's an excellent way to let you know there is more awesome content as long as you keep reading.

This book is filled with a massive number of promises. How many different pieces of content, images, and links did I say would be on the 20K page? Did I promise to include something later in the book? Did I promise to explain something via email?

During this first phase, create a tracking sheet of every loop you open and promise you make. Since I reorder my chapters frequently, it would be easy to accidentally move the close of the loop in front of the opening. When this happens, I need to adjust that promise, or it will be weird for the reader.

How strange would it be if I promised to talk about dictation in the next chapter? I already talked about dictation, but maybe in the original order the dictation section came after the editing chapters. Changing your chapter order risks continuity mistakes. During this stage, make sure that your book flows correctly and adapt to any chapters you move around.

Once you have a list of promises and loops, check to make sure that you complete them. I have a big list of things to add to the 20K page right now. Sometimes I make a promise in a book and then forget about it. Only by keeping a separate list do I ensure that I meet my obligations to every reader.

When you are taking time off between finishing your rough draft and editing, you can work on your promises. When I take my break from writing this book, I will work on the 20K page. I'm using my time productively while allowing my brain to recalibrate.

Often I will ask a friend, customer or intern to go through my book and make a big list of promises. This is a win for both of us. They get early access to my book, and they are far more likely to notice every promise and loop. You don't need a professional editor to make this list; anybody who likes your work can do it.

For many authors, the story ends on the final page of the book. Once they write that page, they can wipe their hands at the end of a job well done. I don't see books that way. When I write a book, that is just the beginning. I want to go beyond our current relationship. I want you to be more than just a reader of this book.

I created the 20K page to encourage you to form a relationship with me; to see us as long-term partners that can work together to make your dreams come true. I want you to email me, follow me on social media and comment on my blog posts. The more we interact, the better. That's why I created the 20K page with so much additional content.

Filling your book with links doesn't benefit the reader or the writer. Trying to upload my pictures of the double rainbow into Kindle format would give you a weaker experience. Would you enjoy a low-resolution, black and white photograph of a rainbow? How annoying is it when you see a link in a book and have to find that link later and write it by hand into your browser?

Providing a secondary location with all your images, videos, bonus content and links is a benefit to your reader. They don't have to try and remember every link you mention. You know that any link or product I mention can be found at ServeNoMaster.com/20k. You only have to remember one link to find all that information; that's easy.

As you visit that page and interact with my website and free content, we will develop a stronger relationship. I love when people send in questions about chapters or point out mistakes in my books. They give me great ways to improve my books for the next readers.

I want to continue to improve my content, and the only way to do that is by connecting with the audience. I fill my books with promises to encourage that connection.

The promise page for *Serve No Master* is nearly 10,000 words. It's 10 percent the length of the entire book. That's a massive amount of bonus content. I made a lot of promises in that book, and it took that many words to keep them.

In each of my books, I make different promises. Each book has a unique page to keep all those promises, and it's critical that I don't miss any. Every promise must be kept, and every loop must be closed. This provides both logical consistency and integrity.

Don't think that this step is only for nonfiction writers. Have you ever watched a movie where a character had two scenes and then seemed to walk off the set of the film? Something happened with a character, and you couldn't wait to see where that story was going? Fiction stories can leave open loops and broken promises as well.

With our list of promises and a rough draft, we have what we need to move on to the next step. You can go back and forth between your book and the promise page, or you can do them separately. Either technique works fine.

Once I finish this step, I'm ready to start using tools to edit.

Action Steps

1. Take a break after finishing your book. Read another book and take enough time off to reset your palate.

2. Organize all of your editing tools and resources, from mind maps to character sheets.

3. Reorganize your chapters to improve the flow and structure of your book.

4. Make a "loops and promises" sheet. Check that you close every loop and fulfill every promise.

5. Start building a promise page to encourage your readers to visit your website and forge a relationship with you.

EDITING STAGE TWO - GRAMMARLY

A philosopher once said, 'Half of good philosophy is good grammar.'
  - A.P. Martinich

The First Tool

The first tool in my editing process is Grammarly. I love this piece of software and could write an entire book on how it has changed my life as a writer. I have already written a 6,000-word review of Grammarly on my blog. Allow me to share some of the highlights here.

Grammarly is an editor that lives inside your computer. It catches many of the mistakes that my line editor finds - long sentences, repeated phrases, and boring structures. I can upload my entire book as a Word document and work through a Grammarly edit in a few hours.

With Scrivener, I copy and paste each section into the Grammarly app and edit one small section at a time. Depending on how much I'm rewriting while I edit, I will use one technique or the other.

This amazing software catches a lot of the mistakes that I miss and has improved the quality of my writing. Every week Grammarly sends a report letting me know that I'm in the top 1 percent of users. It makes me feel pretty good to know that Grammarly is impressed with my work. There is a massive review on my website where I show a ton of secret tips and tricks I have used to become a Grammarly power user.

Grammarly is one of the best tools in my writing arsenal. In less than a year, I have run over one million words through it. I use it every single day for my business, and I can't praise it enough. This one piece of software will revolutionize your editing process.

Grammarly is a life saver and catches 90 percent of the errors that a good line editor would find. You can save a lot of money on editors when your book has far fewer errors.

Grammarly is awesome, but it is not a replacement for a human editor; it will never catch 100 percent of the mistakes. Grammarly isn't perfect and doesn't realize that some misspellings are intentional. Sometimes I am being artistic or using a particular spelling for a reason. Occasionally it gets caught in a loop and keeps recommending I change two words back and forth infinitely.

It might not be perfect, but it is effective. It will catch majority of your mistakes, and as you're going through an editing session, Grammarly catches your new mistakes on the fly.

Grammarly is like having a helpful assistant or a loyal dog at my side. It's helpful and speeds up the editing process. It even notices when my writing starts to become boring. I prefer to edit and rewrite my rough draft inside Grammarly, killing two birds with one stone.

Don't try to take a dictation file from Dragon and shove it into Grammarly. It doesn't work; I tried. You can't use Grammarly to bypass the cleanup phase, unfortunately.

You can use the free version of Grammarly to create a pretty solid book; however, if you are serious about your writing career, it is worth upgrading to the pro version. When you're generating the volume of a 20K System writer, you will more than get your money's worth. When you run a book through a full Grammarly edit, you can protect your book from a "kiss of death" review.

Action Steps

1. Read my entire Grammarly review on my website. There is a link on the 20K page.

2. Use the link on my website to get the free version of Grammarly.

3. Run a test chapter through Grammarly to get a feel for how it works and do see how it jives with your writing style.

4. When you complete your next book, upgrade to the pro version and protect yourself from bad reviews.

EDITING STAGE THREE - BIG PICTURE

Filmmaking is not about the tiny details. It's about the big picture.
- Ed Wood

Consistency

It is tempting to skip around between editing stages, but please resist that temptation. If you stay the course and follow the 20K Editing process, everything will be much quicker. The 20K Editing System is the fastest way to inoculate your book against negative reviews.

After your first run through Grammarly, you will have a much better rough draft. The rough edges are smoother, and a lot of simple mistakes are gone. Since we write with spellcheck turned off, Grammarly catches all those errors that would have slowed you down in the writing phase.

Maintain the Flow

It is now time for the second stage of line editing, where we look for significant changes or shifts in the book. Grammarly is not going to catch it if I'm inconsistent in one of my promises or if my flow goes off course.

It's also not going to catch if one of your characters changes genders or political affiliations. These little mistakes are obvious to humans, but software won't notice them.

Do a big picture read and look for character shifts. Look for a character doing something strange and changing motivation.

Bootstrap Editing

Most new authors can't afford a line editor. They are expensive and take a long time. Can you afford to lose two months of book sales while paying someone a massive amount of money? Probably not.

I don't want to give all my profits to someone else. More than a few editors have offered to work with me for thousands of dollars. That's not a road I will ever go down. These editors are preying on new authors who have no idea what they are doing.

They are looking for writers who have money from a retirement fund or nice savings account they can raid. These writers think they need a great editor to make it in the writing game and they get taken to the cleaners. Unfortunately, they pay these exorbitant prices without knowing better, and they spend money that they will never recover.

I certainly don't want to diminish the value of an editor, and if an editor is going to take six weeks to do something, then they have to earn six weeks of money, but most editors are just going to throw your book into Grammarly and spend a few days on the book. You have to make your own decision balancing the costs and the benefits, but I only use editors sparingly.

Find and Replace

Some mistakes will need to be fixed throughout your book. You might change a character name, and rather than change that name over and over, we can be strategic. Any time you notice a mistake that you'll have to fix a few times, just add it to a special list. Now is the time to deal with that list.

I can't remember the name of this book. It is either going to be *20K a Day* or *20K in a Day*. That little 'in' doesn't make much of a difference, but I'll look like an idiot if I don't fix that before I release the book.

When I'm going through this edit, I type "20K" in the search bar and every time I use that phrase will come up. This will allow me to check that I am consistent about capitalizing the S in 20K System as well.

Some of your changes might affect the physics within your book. If you alter the rules of magic in the final chapter, you need to go back through and correct that continuity error. Trying to fix this type of problem in the middle of your early edits will be a hassle. You can easily miss a spot. Now is the time to go back in and fix any errors from your little list of discontinuities.

One Character at a Time

Once you have completed your list, go through your draft and make each of those changes. This is a great time to double-check all your scientific references and organize your links.

When writing fiction, you can easily find all the scenes for a particular character with your scene map and timeline. You can work on each scene by character until you have the necessary continuity.

Breaking my book into tiny sections pays off at this stage. I try to break up my Scrivener document into the smallest pieces possible. This makes it easy to isolate anything I need to modify, instead of having to dig through a 5,000-word paragraph. Those descriptive section titles make it easy for me to track the sections I need to work on within my book.

I may change all of the chapter names once the book is complete, but the section titles are initially there as guideposts for the writer, not the reader.

Action Steps

1. Look for changes you made in Editing Phases One and Two. Clear up problems with continuity.

2. Edit by character, rather than timeline. Follow each scene that a character is in and ensure their behavior and motivation stays consistent.

3. Use Find and Replace to make any changes that appear in multiple chapters.

4. Organize all your footnotes, endnotes, links and any other references.

5. Keep your overly descriptive section names to find what you need to modify easily.

EDITING STAGE FOUR - LINE EDIT

I put myself in the place of the listener when editing my writing. The last thing that I want to do is be preached at and told who to be or what to think when listening to an artist. However, I do want to be inspired. There's a fine line.

- Macklemore

Get Reading

After grappling with the big picture stuff, it's time for a readthrough. For me, this is where I'm getting closer to what a copy editor does. In the first three phases, I'm not as stressed about spelling and grammar; I only check for the mistakes Grammarly highlights and look for major structural problems or missing sections. I'm not doing a deep read, but more of a scan. These phases should be very quick.

For this entire book, my first pass through Grammarly took less than two hours. I certainly couldn't read this book that fast. The first passes are focused on the forest, rather than the trees. Focus on big picture issues and problems that need to be corrected across your entire manuscript.

Now that those passes are completed, we can start going in deep. It's time to check out those trees.

Zoom in on the Trees

It's time to dig in to the readthrough phase. I like to put a few days between my big picture edit and my first readthrough. Giving my mind a few days to reset allows me to edit with some fresh eyes. Wait at least forty-eight hours between phases.

You don't want to mingle your editing mindsets or get distracted by remembering different versions of a section. A clean palate makes editing much easier.

In the readthrough, I dig deep into my book and look for the tiniest of grammatical and spelling mistakes. You might even catch some big picture mistakes that slipped through. Add any of those to your big picture to-do list and make sure to circle back and check them in a follow-up scan.

This process should be similar to your writing speed. If you are writing 20,000 words per day, you should be able to read through at the same speed. It should take longer than any of the previous editing stages because we are getting very close to the final draft.

It may take multiple readthroughs to get your draft finalized. I try to do as much of my editing in Scrivener, even at this stage. I want my Scrivener file to be my master proof.

Editors tend to charge for each pass through. Even professional editors must read a book two or three times to catch every mistake, so you're going to see new mistakes each time you read through your book no matter what. Mistakes are inevitable, and even if you pay a top-of-the-line editor to go through your book, some mistakes will make it into your final draft. There are many grey areas with grammar and you can find two experts who disagree on the same point. No matter how many editors you hire, there will always be someone who disagrees with some of your decisions.

Rules of grammar are always in flux. The rules I learned in the United States in the nineties are not the same rules kids learn in school now. They are also not the same rules that my older sister learned in the eighties. Slang changes and rules get broken. Don't aim for flawless grammar, just aim for almost perfect.

The goal with editing is not to please everyone, because this is an impossible goal, but instead to avoid getting a "kiss of death" review.

Get Close

The readthrough is not about making big changes, changing the motivation of a character, or moving the location of certain scenes. It's more about looking for small things, making sure that words are spelled correctly, and that characters speak to each other in a consistent way.

We're really in the detail work now looking for little mistakes. That's why this is a slower process. The first process is very rough, like big construction, so you can approach it quite roughly. Now we want to be more detailed. We want to make sure we catch every single mistake and go through it in great detail.

There are other tools that you can use during this process. You may prefer to wait until this point to bring Grammarly into the picture, and that's okay. You can also use a tool called Hemingway, which is far lower priced. Hemingway simply checks for run-on sentences or points when your writing gets boring. It's a little more specific and does one of the things Grammarly does, but it does it very well. Any sentence that is too long or boring, Hemingway will highlight in bright colors until you shorten it.

Action Steps

1. Look for tiny grammatical and spelling mistakes.

   2. Set aside the same amount of time to edit as you did to write.

   3. Save any big picture changes as stick notes.

4. Use Grammarly, Hemingway and any other software tools to help you with this phase.

EDITING STAGE FIVE - THE FIRST REWRITE

The research is the easiest. The outline is the most fun. The first draft is the hardest, because every word of the outline has to be fleshed out. The rewrite is very satisfying.
- Ken Follett

Good to Great

The rewrite is a critical part of the writing process that some authors don't like to talk about. The rewrite is where my books go from good to great. I could have skipped this stage and released *20K a Day* into the world. My first beta reader saw the book at this stage and he completed his first book less than ten days later. That's the ultimate confirmation that the book is ready; it already worked for someone.

I don't want to publish a book that's pretty good. When something is out in the world with my name on it, I want it to be mind-bending. I want you to be so impressed with my work that you feel compelled to email me, draw pictures, and record videos. The rewrite is where that happens.

This book was pretty good after the first five editing stages, but now it's something far more. I have faith that anyone can apply the 20K System and make a living as a writer after reading this book. Hopefully, you feel the same way.

Editing with an Ax

Now, the first readthrough is complete, and you have read the entire book. We are a little closer to the experience our final readers will have, and there will be scenes that you hate and sections that you feel are missing. I can't tell you right now what I'll decide to add to this book during my rewrite phase; I can only tell you that it's going to happen.

In one of my most successful books, when I initially sent it to my publisher, he did a quick scan through it and sent me five sentences of notes. I ended up writing 75 percent more content. I changed the order and did a massive rewrite.

We will talk about honored reviewers and beta readers shortly, but you may want to wait for outside opinions before you start rewriting. [Did you notice that even this late in the book I am still opening loops to encourage you to finish the whole book?]

Serve No Master went through two massive rewrites before I released it. The first rewrite was based on my editing and the second was based on a brutal email from a beta reader. The knife of her review carved that book into a beautiful diamond.

The Cutting Room Floor

During the rewrite stage, you're going to go through your book and write new sections. You may decide to change the order of things. Sometimes you'll delete entire paragraphs or entire chapters.

There are times when we introduce a character that we're very excited about, and in the final version of the book, the character is no longer relevant. They become extraneous. Sometimes you see this in movies where a character seems to have walked off the set of the movie in the first twenty minutes, and you think, "Why was that character even there? They've disappeared."

Sometimes a movie has a character that seems important, and then they spend the rest of the film in their apartment while everyone else is doing stuff. When you notice these things happening in your story, when you notice that you have an extra character or a scene that no longer makes sense, something must change.

I still change the endings in all of my books. During every edit, I change the ending because the book is a living thing. When I get to the end I realize, "Oh, that character I introduced, I need to change him. I don't need him anymore."

When you write those sections and then change them, that's OK. That's what you do during the rewrite. Some stories get cut from a book, and you save those pieces to use in the next book in the series. Don't get emotional about removing a section if the book will be better without it.

It's Not Murder

By rewriting, you're not killing what you wrote before; you're just making it a little better. This is an important part of the process, and it is time-intensive. Rewriting by dictation is nearly impossible. I went through every editing phase of this book by hand.

Give yourself time to rewrite properly. Sometimes the rewrite will take longer than the first rough draft.

I wrote all 93,000 words of *Serve No Master* in four days, but editing it took me four weeks. I have refined my editing process since then. However, the rewrite always takes the longest. If I were to edit that book again, it would take me about one-third the time.

The only way to improve your editing is to do it. We learn through experience, and with each book I write, I continue to improve my process. My goal is to edit as quickly as I write. I want your book to hit the shelves as quickly as possible.

Action Steps

1. Disconnect yourself emotionally from your book. You may need to cut scenes and characters to create a superior finished product.

2. Set aside most of your editing time for this phase. The rewrite is where you take your book from good to great.

3. You may have to edit with an axe. Like a sculptor with a chisel, you are cutting free the fantastic book within that marble.

EDITING STAGE SIX - PROOFREAD YOUR BOOK

Books aren't written - they're rewritten. Including your own. It is one of the hardest things to accept, especially after the seventh rewrite hasn't quite done it.

- Michael Crichton

Reader Experience

Understanding the reader experience is crucial. At some point during your editing process, you'll feel comfortable enough with your book to move into this phase. You may need to cycle through the previous stages a few times before you transition to proofing.

When you feel like your book is nearly ready for release, it's time to proofread. You should read the book in the same way as your customers. If you are selling digital books on Amazon and you don't own a Kindle, you have a serious problem. It can be corrected for under $100.

Whenever I talk to an author who doesn't own a Kindle, I am very disappointed. How can you know what the reader experience is like?

You have to check what your book looks like on Kindle. You have to see how the formatting looks, how the artistry looks, and look for mistakes that aren't apparent until you load the book into a Kindle.

Many authors skip the proofreading stage because they don't know what it means. Many people think that proofreading and editing are interchangeable words, but they are not.

You need to read the book in the same format as your audience. You need to see what they see.

Kettle of Fish

I read books on my Kindle every day. The rhythm of a story is always fresh and makes it easy to have that flow in my stories. You must own a Kindle if you want people to read your books on one. You need to experience your book in the same way as your customers. Many books look beautiful printed, but on a Kindle, they look like garbage.

As authors, we put in all this artistry without realizing that it gets destroyed by the Kindle. I know quite a few authors who were surprised to discover that a reader can change the size of the text on a Kindle. I use the second largest size, but plenty of people use the largest size, and I'm sure some prefer the tiniest font size. Each of those people has a different reader experience than I do.

When I look at a Kindle page, there are about 125 words. I read those 125 words and push a button to go to the next page. That's my reader experience. Some people see fifty words on the page, and some people see 200 or 300.

If you don't know that, you'll run into problems. The number of people who don't know that Kindle books are black and white blows my mind. Many book covers look cool in color and atrocious in black and white. Some writers don't know that people with Kindles make most of their purchases via the device. I acquire 90 percent of my books via my Kindle, so that's how I know that the cover has to look good in black and white. If you don't have a Kindle, you won't notice these little differences.

First Kindle Proof

There are two ways you can proofread your digital book. First, download an app, like Calibre, which will load your book directly onto your Kindle. This is the preferred method for your first proofread and beta readers, which we will cover in the next chapter.

Reading your book inside a Kindle will catch a lot of mistakes. When reading your book, highlight anything you want to change. As I read through my draft, I save every mistake as a highlight. I highlight the entire sentence around any mistake that I catch.

When I finish the proofread, I can open up the highlights and notes from that book in my device. I have a big list of everything I need to go and correct. Highlighting the entire sentence makes it easy for me to use the "find" feature in my word processor to locate each problem.

Proofreading using the highlight feature is pretty cool. I was very excited when I figured this out. When proofreading on a Kindle, you don't want to run to your computer to correct each mistake. It knocks you out of the zone and takes too long. With highlighting, you can read your book in bed, on your couch, or even sitting by the seaside.

It's always amazing to me how many mistakes I find reading my own book in bed. But that's why we proofread.

Final Kindle Proof

The second way to proof your book is to upload it to Amazon and then purchase a copy. Only do this when you feel as though the book is ready to launch. This step is absolutely critical and I can't stress this enough.

Amazon reformats your book before sending it through their system. Even the proof you transferred directly to your Kindle won't be exactly the same as the version your customers receive.

When checking this final proof, I'm mostly looking for big formatting mistakes. I'm not checking spelling. Amazon arbitrarily sets the "start page" for your book. If you never check, your readers might be missing where you want them to start.

In one of my earlier books, Amazon put the start page after my free gift page. I couldn't understand why nobody was submitting their email addresses. Only when I proofread the book as a customer did I find and correct this error.

There are a few other mistakes that I see in books I read on Amazon. Many authors upload maps, diagrams and images to their books incorrectly. There is nothing more annoying than an image file that I can't see inside a book. I have seen this with successful authors as well as independent authors.

You need to check how your images look inside a Kindle. You can't rely on Amazon to get everything right. As the saying goes, "Trust, but verify."

KDP Print Edit

Before you start sending out paperback copies of your book, proof it. KDP Print will send you a copy of your book for under ten bucks, and it's worth every penny. When you upload a book to KDP Print, you can order a full proof before making the book available for sale. I love this feature.

Because I live on the other side of the world, I can't proof my physical books. KDP Print provides me with a PDF that looks just like my physical book. I spend a long time with this final proof, checking how images look and tracking the blocking.

I catch a lot of mistakes with the PDF proof that somehow slipped through the cracks. Seeing a book in this format is informative.

When editing a physical copy of your book, just highlight, circle, or underline anything you want to correct. Once you have finished reading the whole book, sit down at your computer and fix each error.

Action Steps

1. Download an app to transfer your draft to a Kindle.

2. Proofread your book on a Kindle (or whichever digital reader you want your customers to use).

3. Get a KDP Print proof.

4. Proofread the entire book and make a list of corrections, then go back to your computer and work your way through your list.

5. Check the start and end of your book and any images or maps.

6. After you upload your book to Amazon or any other bookstore, be the first customer and perform your final proofread.

BETA READERS

I want my stories to be understood and enjoyed by anyone, so I need 'beta-readers' who will tell me when the plot is working or not working, and when my writing is concise or vague.
  - Tony DiTerlizzi

Your Loyal Army

It's time to start sharing your book with fans outside of your family. There are two types of people who see early copies of my book: beta readers and early reviewers. These terms are not interchangeable.

An early reviewer gets a copy of the book during the proofreading phase. They will see a book that is very close to being finished. I mainly want them to leave me positive feedback and maybe catch a few tiny errors that have slipped through the cracks.

A beta reader will see the book even earlier. A beta reader gets a copy of the book knowing that it's not complete. Depending upon how early I send a copy to a beta reader, I may ask them to ignore grammar, spelling or even the order of chapters. Later phase beta readers will pay more attention to these issues and send the appropriate feedback.

Advance Review Copies

During this phase where I'm reading as a reader, I often also send out copies to my loyal early reviewers. Depending upon the source you have for early readers, you can send a rougher version for certain websites that I use, and I have links to all those places to get early readers. But they will be brutal towards you for sending them a version that's not completely finished.

Whereas my inner circle, my loyal readers, I can send them a version and say, "This is the rough draft. I want to send it to you before anyone else. I'm editing it right now, so if you catch anything I miss, please tell me." Ninety percent of the people you interact with will be OK with this.

Some people I can send the entire message, and they'll still be like, "This book isn't finished. How dare you!" And even when I say, "Well I gave you a free book and I told you it wasn't finished," they still get grouchy.

It just depends. This is something we deal with as authors. We learn from the people we deal with how we can find good and bad readers, and what the experiences are like.

Not every reader and reviewer you get will be great, but many of your early reviewers will be helpful. Usually when you send out 200 early copies, only five of the people will get back to you.

What those few send you will be pure gold and make it worth the other people who completely ignored you and just took a free copy. Don't worry about that stuff.

Give 'em Time

I'm an insanely fast reader. I can read hundreds of pages in a single day, but most people aren't like this. Beta readers take their job seriously, so they read even slower than usual. Many beta readers will take notes as they read. They are awesome, and you can't rush them.

Some beta readers and reviewers might take months to finish their readthrough. Even though the feedback or review comes in six months after I released the book, I will go through and correct all the mistakes they caught. I am always looking to improve my books, even after release.

I try to send out beta copies at least two weeks before I plan on publishing a book. This gives them plenty of time to finish and send feedback before that date. Not everyone will finish in that time and I'm totally fine with that. As long as two or three of my readers do, I will have a really tight final draft on launch day.

Where to Find Them

Finding beta readers for your first novel can feel like a bit of the chicken and the egg. You can't find readers until you publish the book, but you can't publish the book until you've had some beta readers.

Some editors offer beta-reading, and it's not too expensive. A beta reader for a 100,000-word book could be under $100. That's afford-able for most new writers and won't crush your bank account.

There are a few places to find beta readers without spending any money. There are beta reader groups on Goodreads and Facebook. There are also a few platforms where writers critique each other to share the love. As you leave more critiques, your earn points and people will return the favor. I will leave links to more places to find beta readers on the 20K page as I discover them.

When you are using a stranger for a beta reader, the book should be as far as you can take it on your own. Don't send a draft with broken grammar to one of these readers; they should receive a version of your book that is after at least one rewrite.

Action Steps

1. Find at least twenty potential beta readers.

2. Join three beta reader groups.

3. Join Scribophile and start earning points by critiquing other authors. Build up your points before you need them.

4. Send out the best draft you can to twenty beta readers and wait for feedback over the next two weeks.

5. Give very clear instructions about what feedback you are looking for.

HONORED REVIEWERS

Reviewers are the worst laughers in the world.
  - Chris O'Dowd

Trusted Friends

An early reviewer is someone that you can send a final draft of your book to. When you send out a copy of your book, it should be good enough that people will leave positive reviews. You are not focused on error-correction anymore. You want to build a little buzz for your book.

Early reviewers might catch a few mistakes here and there, but that is not their primary purpose. Most early reviewers should give your book a five-star review. If they don't think your book is worthy, they should email you and explain why. Then you can fix those mistakes before the general public gets their hands on your book.

Don't bother asking your friends and family to be early reviewers and editors. They are too close to you, and you won't get the feedback you need. Most people will pretend your book is fine just to avoid an uncomfortable conversation. They would rather avoid that awkwardness than point out any significant problems in your book. I never ask friends and family for reviews; Amazon doesn't allow it anymore anyway.

Early Readers

I have some very dedicated fans who I love very much. There are certain people that I send free copies of my books to. People who leave great reviews on Amazon get invited to become early reviewers, and if they do a great job, they get invited to be beta readers.

To get onto my radar, just leave a detailed, high-quality review of one of my books and then email me. I get one or two emails a week like this. I keep track of them, and they are my honored reviewers.

Anytime a reviewer e-mails me, I reply. I look at their blogs and writing projects and share some feedback with them. Some of my reviewers work their way up through my product chain. I have products that are very expensive. My top training programs cost thousands of dollars. A good reviewer can work their way through my entire product line without spending a penny.

When a reviewer leaves valuable reviews, records videos, and sends me private feedback when they see a mistake on my website, they get moved up a tier in my honored reviewer program. You should reward your readers in the same way. Every time you see a great review on Amazon, click on the reviewer's profile. Many of them include a link to social media or an email account. You should reach out and thank that reviewer to start the relationship.

Some early reviewers are amazingly critical. One of the early reviewers for my first set of Blueprints had me tearing my hair out daily. He is like a mistake-finding missile. No matter how small the error, he catches every single one. But when he has finished going through a product, I have absolute faith that it's flawless.

Fix Every Mistake

Most early reviewers will email you their feedback rather than leave a bad review. They know that you are early in the creative process and will help you improve your book. It's much better to get any criticisms via email.

There's nothing worse than putting a book on Amazon and then finding out there's a terrible mistake or receiving a brutal one-star review that you spend the rest of your career trying to recover from.

Sending out review copies is critical. As long as you are at least two weeks pre-launch, you will have time to correct any of the errors that come in. Sometimes you send out an early copy only a week before your release date. In this case, reviewers might not get back to you until after your book is live, but you can still make changes before most readers see your book.

Using Kindle and KDP Print, you can make changes to your books on the fly. As soon as someone sends in a mistake to me, I go and fix both my digital and physical editions. I update both versions, knowing that no one who purchases the book after this point will see those mistakes.

Early reviewers are worth their weight in gold. Their feedback will make your book magnificent. They will find mistakes that you might not see on a dozen readthroughs. You don't have to wait until you start selling your book to get people to read it.

I usually ask my early reviewers to email me all their feedback. After the book is live, I ask all the people who sent me great feedback to copy and paste it into a review on Amazon. This will help give your next book a little boost. Launching your book with a few positive reviews will give you a major advantage over the competition.

No matter how many times you read your book, you are always going to find tiny mistakes and sentences you want to change. Even a year after release, I get emails about *Serve No Master*, where someone notices a little mistake that 10,000 other readers missed. They catch where you used a period instead of a comma or where there are two spaces between words instead of one.

Sometimes it Hurts

There's nothing worse than thinking you have finished your book, only to discover that you're not even close.

After my first rewrite of *Serve No Master*, I sent out the early release copies. I was on the ball this time and sent out these copies a few weeks before my launch date. A few reviewers pointed out tiny grammatical mistakes, but on the whole the feedback was all positive. Except for one email:

Hi Jonathan,

Thank you for book, which I am super excited about reading. Time is running short for your launch day and I wanted to let you know that I have noticed a lot of grammatical errors, and I've only reached page 41. I don't have the time to highlight them all for you unfortunately, not before your launch day. And besides, that is not what you want from me as a reviewer any way. Editing is a time-consuming endeavor and it isn't something I would do for free! Not on this large a scale...

I'm loving your style and anecdotes so far and finishing your book is on my top priority list this week, however, at this stage, I don't see how I will be able to give you a five-star review with so many errors. :-(which is frustrating because that is the least important thing really, content is the key and so far you're killing it.

Anyway I wanted to give you a big heads up so you can go through it again before launch day.

Out of 200 reviewers, this is the one that still sticks in my mind nearly a year later. After reading this email, I wanted to curl up into the fetal position and spend a few hours crying.

I had two choices: pretend I hadn't seen this email and launch my book as it was, or do something. I chose action.

I purchased Grammarly ten minutes later and spent the next thirty-six hours editing and rewriting nearly every one of those 94,000 words. I lost track of time, and my cortex nearly fused. This email came in on Monday, and the book was scheduled for release on Saturday.

I decided to do whatever it took to turn this negative review into a positive. This was a learning experience that I hope you never have to repeat. When I came out the other side, my book was far better, and I improved my editing process. That book has been a massive success, and I credit a large part of that to this brutal email.

Seeking Criticism

With your early reviewers, you are looking to rack up some positive reviews for your book launch, but you also want them to point out any mistakes that have slipped through the cracks. Do not attach any emotion to your book at this point.

When you get a negative review, it's tempting to react emotionally. You want to lash out and tell the reader that they are an idiot and wouldn't know good literature if it slapped them in the face. You might be right, but that is not productive. Don't let a bad review hurt your feelings. If you need to cry for a few hours, do that and get it out of your system. Then pick yourself back up and improve your book.

The editing is the toughest part of this entire process. It can feel like you are judging your work and letting others determine if you are worthy. Don't get caught up in that mindset. The book is not complete until you publish it. The end of the first draft is just that, a draft.

If you think of beta readers and early reviewers as part of the creative process, you will save yourself from a lot of emotional turmoil.

Action Steps

1. Build a list of early reviewers.

2. Head over to the 20K page to find more resources for finding early reviewers.

3. Organize all your early reviewers so that you can easily contact them about your next book.

4. Prepare yourself emotionally for criticism and use it to forge your book into something amazing.

HIRING AN EDITOR

Most of my success, I feel, comes from being a good editor as opposed to a great writer.
    - Tucker Max

Dollars to Donuts

The editor question comes down to one of finances. If you can afford an editor and at a reasonable price, go for it. Your book will come out the other side far better than it went in.

I usually wait until I'm at the end of my process before bringing in an editor. I don't want to pay someone to fix all my grammatical mistakes only to realize that I need to rewrite a few chapters. For me, the editor is the final polish. The editor is the last person who sees my book before I release it into the world. My editor is the final gatekeeper.

I don't use an editor for every book that I release, but for my larger releases, I like to bring in a professional. I don't want a book about writing to have mistakes in it. I know that you'll give me a brutal review if it does.

The Final Edit

The last thing I do before publishing a book is send it to my editor. If he's busy and can't look at a book until after the release date, I don't push back my launch. I can update the book a few weeks after publishing it and most of my readers will never notice.

Most editors and proofreaders will edit a sample of your book ranging from 500 to 1,000 words. You can find a few editors using the links on the 20K page and find one with a style you like.

Be clear about your expectations upfront. I want an editor to fix all the grammatical, spelling and punctuation mistakes. For content editing, I usually rely on my early readers. They will let me know if sections are missing or parts of the book are boring.

When my editor is finished going through my manuscript, he will send back a Word document with every change marked. Word has a featured called "track changes" that lets you see every modification made to a document. Once I receive this file, I go through and manually approve each change. I then copy each section back into Scrivener, and now I have my final proof.

My editor is as fast as me and can process around 20,000 words a day. He edited *Breaking Orbit* in under forty-eight hours, and he'll be editing this book as well.

The ultimate test of any editor is your readers. If you get bad grammar reviews after hiring an editor, don't use them again. I have yet to receive an email or review pointing out errors in *Breaking Orbit*. That's the ultimate proof that my editor is amazing.

Action Steps

1. Track your finances and establish a budget for an editor based on how much money you have now, not on predicted sales.

2. Check out a few links to editors from the 20K page.

3. Bring in an editor only after your early reviewers have sent in their feedback.

4. If you can't afford an editor at this point, that's ok. The 20K Editing Process will protect you from "kiss of death" reviews.

WISDOM FOR NEW
WRITERS

The journey of a thousand miles begins with one step.
   - Lao Tzu

Listen to the Feedback

A few early reviewers and coaching clients sent in some questions that didn't really fit anywhere else in the book. This chapter is a collection of my final words of wisdom before launching you out into the world as a 20K writer.

Author or Seller

Plenty of books out there will tell you to write about any topic as long as you are passionate about it. And while writing something is better than writing nothing, I don't believe in this advice. I would never be the first person to write about a brand-new topic. If you want to be creative and write a book backward or put the chapters out of order, then I'm not the person to come to for advice. I can think of a few great movies that use this technique. But they are the exception, not the rule.

Misspelling words or creating strange meanings to add a bit of whimsy to your work can overwhelm your readers. Only amazing authors can use these types of techniques effectively, and I am not one of them. I'm not an ivory tower author. I'm out in the streets, getting dirty and writing with my fists. I don't have a silver tongue.

There is a lot of advice out there for authors. You should only take advice from someone you are in alignment with. If you think my writing is pedestrian and that I don't use enough multisyllabic words, then you shouldn't follow my systems. Find a leader who writes the way you want to.

This book is about writing fast, but it's also about so much more. It's part of my entire *Serve No Master* series. It's part of a larger structure. As much as this book is about writing fast, it's about writing books that will sell and that people will read.

I want you to make money from the books you write. My previous book in the series, *Breaking Orbit*, teaches you how to publish a book and launch a bestseller on Amazon. This book is designed to dovetail with that.

This book is so long because I want to share everything I know about writing fast with you. But that is not enough. I don't want you to be a struggling artist. What good is writing fast if you can't pay the bills? I know that you want to write fast as a means to an end. This book is about hitting your real goal.

Are You Not Entertained?

If you start with an idea without doing any market research, you can use the 20K System to write a book very quickly. Unfortunately, you might not sell a single copy, and I want to prepare you for that possibility.

We are near the end of this book but I don't want you to forget the beginning. My method for writing is very simple: find out what people want and give it to them. Researching before you write ensures that there is an audience ready and waiting to read your book. There are certain topics that do amazing in the direct response realm and do terribly on Amazon.

I don't write relationship books for Amazon because no one buys them. It's not a market where people buy a lot of relationship books. People always want to break into the relationships space on Amazon, but there is simply no money to be made. That's not where most people buy their advice these days.

Some authors out there will say, "Hey, write about whatever you want to write about," and I think that's very disingenuous. You can write about whatever you want, but be aware that if you write about a topic in a brand-new way that no one likes, you might not have any readers, and it can be very lonely out there.

Sometimes authors join my coaching group with a book already published. They released a book five or ten years ago and have sold less than a dozen copies in that time; they are not happy.

Who wants to write a book that no one reads? As much as I think it's a tool to get people motivated, the whole "Write whatever you feel like. Trust your instincts," thing takes it too far. It's going to leave you disappointed in the end.

I'm more interested in your end result. I can make you happy right now or happy long-term, and I'd rather you write a book series that people like. Whether you're writing fiction or nonfiction, research is critical. Before I write the first word of an outline, I want to see people on Amazon interested in the topic. I only write books for categories where there is enough money to be made for it to be worth my time.

I mentioned earlier that I wanted to write a book about email marketing. I didn't intend to cover this topic until next year. I hadn't even considered a book on writing fast, dictation, and my editing process.

I was excited about writing a book on email marketing because I've been thinking about it a lot over the last month and working on some big email projects. In my research, I discovered that no one cares. Books about email marketing don't sell on Amazon. If I wrote the best email book in the world, the profit would be around $100 per month. That is just not worth my time right now.

Later on down the line in the series, I might cover the topic, but for now the books I write are driven by my readers' passion, not my own.

It doesn't make sense to write a book that no one wants to read.

Build the Editing Habit

If you are a creative person like me, you will discover that editing is far harder than writing. I would much rather write. During the editing process, you must be very strict with your emotions. Remember those chapters on habit.

When you get upset at errors in the book or a negative email from an early reviewer, you are falling into that trap again. Do not attach negative emotions to any part of this process. If you attach a negative emotion to early reviewer emails, you'll stop sending out early review copies. Better to publish an incomplete book than get a bunch of emails hurting your feelings.

Attach positive emotions to the act of trying. Every time you put in effort, you should feel good about yourself. You should say, "I did a good thing. I tried hard and I'm proud of myself."

Train yourself to think this way, and you will become a limitless author. You will write amazing books and continue to improve with every word you write.

Be proud when you catch a mistake. Don't focus on not catching it earlier. You found it now, and nothing else matters.

Let's say you're on the final edit and it's the day before the book comes out. You find a mistake in the first sentence of your book; you used a comma when you should have used a semi-colon. You could say to yourself, "I'm such a loser. I forgot. I missed this. I can't believe I missed this. I'm not a real author." Or you could say, "I'm proud of myself because I caught this before the book went live." We can apply a positive spin every time we run into an error.

Do not turn random errors into systemic problems. Even big

mistakes and plot holes do not make you a terrible writer. Do not question your writing or call yourself bad words.

Remember what I've taught you and always attach a positive emotion. Say to yourself, "I tried and caught this mistake now before it's too late. I did a good job. That's all that matters." The more you can do that, the more you will succeed.

Even if you get a bad review six months after publishing your book, use that as a learning experience. Fix that mistake and make your next book even better.

Trust Your Instincts

There will be parts of your book that you are on the fence about. You can't decide if that section is good or if you should chop it out. Maybe you need to rewrite a chapter. You think, "I kind of like this, but it's not great." This happens to all of us. Whenever I have one of these, I send that to someone and 99 percent of the time they'll say, "That part's terrible."

If you are unsure about a part of your book, most likely your audience will hate it. Trust your first instinct. Almost all of my negative feedback is about things I was unsure of myself.

This is when you'll catch those big mistakes. We have this tendency to notice things that are fifty-fifty and think, "I'm not sure if I want to keep that or not." And then when we think about it, we go, "Oh, I'm probably just overanalyzing. I'm being overly critical of myself. I'm a perfectionist." Our first instinct catches the mistake but then our second instinct stops us from fixing it.

Trust your first instinct more than your second instinct. Whenever you have one of these moments, err on the side of making a change. Bring in an outside opinion to confirm, but be ready to fix it.

Over time, you'll discover that your first instinct is pretty much always right. Because I read books every day I have a strong feel for story flow. When I'm in writing mode, I might not notice a problem with my book's pacing. But when I'm proofreading the final version of my book on a Kindle, I'll catch those tiny errors that were niggling at the back of my brain.

Roll with the Punches

There comes the point that the book goes out into the world, and you will quickly discover that writing is a democracy; every single reader gets a vote. They get to vote with their dollars and with their reviews.

You give your best effort in the book, do everything you can to tighten up the story, and then get as many early readers as you can. When you get a bad review, adapt and update the book. If you need to add in some new sections, do it. If you get a bunch of negative reviews about a particular character in your book, fix them.

If your book is live and you are getting bad reviews, update the book and then change the description. You can say that it's now version 2.0 of the book; it's been updated, and the grammar has been corrected. Make it clear that those bad reviews are about a book that no longer exists. Clean the slate.

I've seen a book description start with, "Now professionally edited and no more grammatical mistakes," because they got a bunch of bad reviews. They used their book profits to hire an editor. If you can't afford an editor upfront, this is a great alternative.

No problem is unfixable. There might be sections in the book where you get stuck. Sometimes you'll feel painted into a corner, and that happens, but you can fight your way out.

The 20K System has a very strict structure for how we prepare, write, and edit so that you can consistently release fantastic books. Stick with the process, and you will write and edit books very quickly. You will be very proud of every book you finish.

Smooth is Fast

Writing faster does not mean writing worse; it does not mean rushing yourself. I never want you to feel pressure or nervousness. Anxiety and stress will damage your writing.

You should never drive a car so fast that you can't see what's happening in front of you. Don't write that fast either. If you can't tell what you're writing about, slow down.

The 20K System is really about speeding up the time between your thoughts and putting words on the page.

As an early writer, I suffered a great deal. That pain forced me to write faster. I had no choice but to become a 20K writer. While I was writing, my thoughts would be several seconds ahead of my hands, and it would drive me crazy. My body and mind were out of sync.

With my thoughts ahead of my hands, I would continually lose my train of thought. I would lose ideas before I could get them onto the page. I would be writing about A and thinking about C, and I would often forget that B idea in the middle. My train of thought was derailing all the time.

As a writer, I was meandering. I felt lost and confused in the desert. I was miserable with my writing process. I trained my hands to write as fast as my brain could think.

Right now you speak much faster than you write. And you think even faster than you speak. The 20K System is about catching your body up to how fast your brain is working. It is not about writing so fast that your quality suffers. You have to write unbelievably fast to outpace your thoughts.

As long as you follow the steps in this process, you will be very successful. Problems occur when you start skipping steps or getting creative. This system is strict because that will maximize your results. Following each step in the correct order will turn you into a 20K writer who can live off the words you write. The order of chapters in this book is not random; stick to the correct order.

Whenever you feel like you are drifting off course, reread that section of this book. Stick with the exercises and systems to get back on track.

Action Steps

1. Jump to the end of this book and leave a five-star review. Uploading pictures or videos is an excellent way to get on my radar and get additional personal advice when you reach out to me.

2. If you noticed any grammatical, spelling, or punctuation mistakes, please email me. Allow me to improve this book for the readers to follow.

3. Make a plan to become a 20K writer. Stick to your plan until you hit your goal.

4. Work your way through all the action steps and exercises in this book.

5. Visit ServeNoMaster.com/20k to find links and a boatload of free bonus content.

6. Grab your free gift before it's gone.

ONE LAST CHANCE

Thank you so much for reading *20K a Day*. In case you missed it at the start of the book, here is my special gift to you. This is a long book and I put together a Top Secret Cheatsheet with all the most valuable information. You can grab it by clicking this link.

ServeNoMaster.com/cheatsheet

FOUND A TYPO?

While every effort goes into ensuring that this book is flawless, it is inevitable that a mistake or two will slip through the cracks.

If you find an error of any kind in this book, please let me know by visiting:

ServeNoMaster.com/typos

I appreciate you taking the time to notify me. This ensures that future readers never have to experience that awful typo. You are making the world a better place.

ABOUT THE AUTHOR

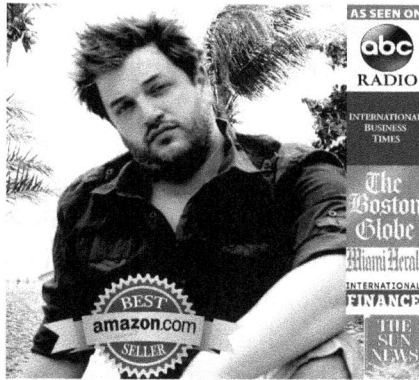

Born in Los Angeles, raised in Nashville, educated in London, Jonathan Green has spent years wandering the globe as his own boss – but it didn't come without a price. Like most people, he struggled through years of working in a vast, unfeeling bureaucracy.

After the backstabbing and gossip of the university system threw him out of his job, he was devastated – stranded far away from home without a paycheck coming in. Despite having to hang on to survival with his fingernails, he didn't just survive; he thrived.

Today, he says that getting fired with no safety net was the best thing that ever happened to him. Despite the stress, it gave him an opportunity to rebuild and redesign his life.

One year after being on the edge of financial ruin, Jonathan had replaced his job, working as a six-figure SEO consultant. With his Rolodex overflowing with local businesses and their demands getting higher and higher, he knew that he had to take his hands off the wheel.

That's one of the big takeaways from his experience. Lifestyle design can't just be about a job replacing income, because often, you're replicating the stress and misery that comes with that lifestyle too!

Thanks to smart planning and personal discipline, he started from scratch again, with a focus on repeatable, passive income that created lifestyle freedom. He was more successful than he could have possibly expected. He traveled the world, helped friends and family, and moved to an island in the South Pacific.

Now, he's devoted himself to breaking down every hurdle entrepreneurs face at every stage of their progress, from developing mental strength and resilience in the depths of depression and anxiety, to developing financial and business literacy, to building a concrete plan to escape the 9-to-5, all the way down to the nitty-gritty details of teaching what you need to build a business of your own.

In a digital world packed with "experts," there are few people with the experience to tell you how things really work, why they work and what actually works in the online business world.

Jonathan doesn't just have the experience; he has it in a variety of spaces. A bestselling author, a "ghostwriter to the gurus" who commands sky-high rates due to his ability to deliver captivating work in a hurry, and a video producer who helps small businesses share their skills with their communities.

He's also the founder of the Serve No Master podcast, a weekly show focused on financial independence, networking with the world's most influential people, writing epic stuff online and traveling the world for cheap.

Altogether, it makes him one of the most captivating and accomplished people in the lifestyle design world, sharing the best of what he knows with total transparency, as part of a mission to free regular people from the 9-to-5 and live on their own terms.

Learn from his successes and failures and Serve No Master.

Find out more about Jonathan at:
ServeNoMaster.com

BOOKS BY JONATHAN GREEN

Non-Fiction

Serve No Master Series

Serve No Master

Breaking Orbit

20K a Day

Control Your Fate

Breakthrough (coming soon)

Habit of Success Series

PROCRASTINATION

Influence and Persuasion

Overcome Depression

Stop Worrying and Anxiety

Love Yourself

Conquer Stress

Law of Attraction

Mindfulness and Meditation Ultimate Guide

Meditation Techniques for Beginners

I'm Not Shy

Coloring Depression Away with Adult Coloring Books

Don't be Quiet

How to Make Anyone Like You

Develop Good Habits with S.J. Scott

How to Quit Your Smoking Habit

The Weight Loss Habit

Seven Secrets

Seven Networking Secrets for Jobseekers

Biographies

The Fate of my Father

Complex Adult Coloring Books

The Dinosaur Adult Coloring Book

The Dog Adult Coloring Book

The Celtic Adult Coloring Book

The Outer Space Adult Coloring Book

The 2nd Celtic Adult Coloring Book

The Stop Smoking Adult Coloring Book

Irreverent Coloring Books

Dragons Are Bastards

Fiction

Gunpowder and Magic

The Outlier (As Drake Blackstone)

ONE LAST THING

When you turn the page, Kindle will give you the option to rate this book and share your thoughts on Facebook and Twitter. If you found value in this book, I would appreciate it if you would take a few seconds and click the FIVE STARS icon and share with your friends. If they desire to write faster, they will be grateful for the recommendation.

Without stars and reviews, you would never have found this book. Please take just thirty seconds of your time to support an independent author by leaving a rating.

Thank you so much!

Sincerely,

Jonathan Green

ServeNoMaster.com